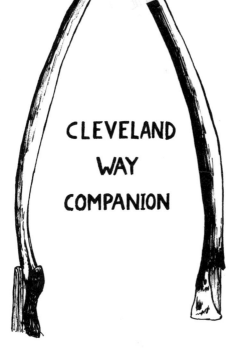

CLEVELAND
WAY
COMPANION

HILLSIDE GUIDES

FREEDOM OF THE DALES
40 selected walks
Full colour hardback

80 DALES WALKS
Omnibus edition of Books 4,6,8,11 and (in part)10,21
Published by Cordee, Leicester

CLEVELAND WAY
COMPANION

by

Paul Hannon

HILLSIDE  PUBLICATIONS

HILLSIDE PUBLICATIONS
11 Nessfield Grove
Exley Head
Keighley
West Yorkshire
BD22 6NU

First published 1986
3rd (Revised) impression 1992

The maps in this book are based upon
the 1895 – 1930 Ordnance Survey 1:10,560 (6") maps

Page 1 illustration
Whalebone arch, West Cliff, Whitby

ISBN   1 870141 17 2

Printed in Great Britain by
Carnmor Print and Design
95/97 London Road
Preston
Lancashire
PR1 4BA

CONTENTS

East Cliff from West Cliff, Whitby

INTRODUCTION

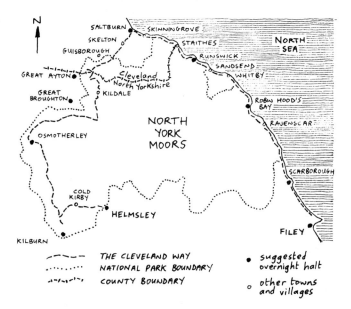

– – – – THE CLEVELAND WAY	• suggested overnight halt
·········· NATIONAL PARK BOUNDARY	
⌐⌐⌐⌐ COUNTY BOUNDARY	○ other towns and villages

The Cleveland Way is a 109 — mile long National Trail in and around the North York Moors National Park, and it was only the second such route to be given official status. The Way's grand opening was at Helmsley, the starting point, in 1969 four years after the Pennine Way was unleashed upon us: in reality however it had been walked for many years previous.

The walk's working title was the North York Moors and Yorkshire Coast Path, a rather prosaic mouthful that fortunately had its opponents. Cleveland was an ancient district which very approximately extended over the northern half of the walk. Ironically the name was reintroduced in 1974 to describe a newly-created county, which to confuse matters only covers a greatly reduced area at the apex of the Way. The remainder of the walk is within North Yorkshire county. That original title suitably described the nature of the walk, for it is indeed a moors and coast path — two highly distinct sections which combine to form a walk of immense variety. Inland, the way treads the high western and northern escarpments of the Hambleton Hills and the Cleveland Hills, leading to the second half of the walk, an unbroken trek along the coast. As so much of the Way is above steep drops and cliffs, how fitting its title is, for the word Cleveland is a derivation of 'cliff-land'.

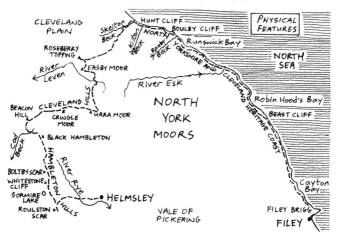

The North York Moors are an exceptionally well-defined area, and the Cleveland Way hugs two sides of the National Park from Helmsley to Scarborough. This 'twinning' with a Park (something only one other 'official' path equals) ensures the scenery is of a sustained high quality.

This near-insular area contains almost as much of historic interest as it does of natural beauty. Within a mile of the Way are the monastic houses of Rievaulx and Mount Grace, while Whitby Abbey is on the route: both Helmsley and Scarborough possess ruined castles. Many of the coastal villages were smugglers' havens, and most survive to some extent still as fishing ports. Old coastguard paths lead along the cliffs past various look-out posts and the sites of old shipwrecks far below. For several miles the Way follows the Hambleton Drove Road north into the heart of Cleveland's old quarrying and mining district, jet, ironstone and alum being the targets. Much evidence of these activities remains, and the latter is particularly conspicuous on the coastline. The district's most famous son was Captain Cook, and the Way visits several sites of related interest. There is a good deal of geological interest notably along the coast, with rich and varied flora and fauna throughout the walk.

PLANNING THE WALK

The Cleveland Way runs from Helmsley to near Filey, a distance of 109 miles which in practice becomes 112 miles on reaching Filey itself. For practical reasons it is usually completed in a week, but longer should be allowed if possible. This guide has been divided into nine daily sections to allow ample time for the numerous distractions which inevitably present themselves.

Ordnance column,
Roseberry Topping

If it is decided to take either less or even more time, then a whole range of permutations of overnight stops is available. To those halts already recommended, Kildale, Guisborough, Staithes and Whitby can be added to give options from seven days to a whole fortnight. Accommodation is scarcer on the inland section.

Of the terminal points, Filey is easily reached by train and by bus from Scarborough. Helmsley is also linked to Scarborough by bus, and to a lesser extent to Thirsk, which has a railway station. A popular practice for those with cars is to motor to Helmsley, leave the car in the car-park near the castle, and return after the walk by bus from Filey via Scarborough. If adopting this method it is advisable to leave a note with the local police.

The path itself is for the most part very clear, and thus easy to follow. Inland the Way makes use of wide moorland and woodland tracks, while on the coast the path is largely self-evident for obvious reasons. Acorn symbols and guideposts assist on many occasions. Instances of footpath erosion due to over-use are relatively few: the major problem is on the Cleveland Hills, where numerous other walks jostle for space on the same 12-mile length.

The paths can become slippy after prolonged rain, and care is needed particularly on the cliff-tops. This is where natural erosion occurs, as the sea pecks incessantly away at our treasured coastline. Although the altitude on the cliffs is of course less than that on the moors, there are a substantial number of short steep pulls from sea-level to the cliff-tops, and with them, corresponding drops.

The walk contains lengthy sections over moor and cliff seemingly far from civilisation, but really there are very few occasions when a road is not fairly close by. Oases of refreshment are few and far between on the inland section and alcoholic sustenance or not, these opportunities are seldom passed up: conversely, the coastal settlements usually offer a choice of such establishments. Few would

argue against late summer being the best time to walk the Cleveland Way, when the heather makes an unforgettable display over vast expanses of rolling moorland. This walk is however through country of such infinite beauty that it is bound to impress, whatever the season.

Since its inception the Cleveland Way has been linked with other long-distance paths, namely the Wolds Way at Filey and the Ebor Way at the Helmsley end. An unofficial route known as the Missing Link was devised by a local man in 1975, and this returns the walker to Helmsley from Crook Ness near Scarborough in three stages: the most useful overnight stops would be Lockton and Hutton-le-Hole. This may well

Captain Cook statue, West Cliff, Whitby

appeal to anyone taking a fortnight off, but the last leg to Filey is worthy of completion first.

Below is a very brief list of books on the area, which provide good background reading before or during the walk. The first three capture the true spirit of the moors.

INSIDE THE NORTH YORK MOORS - Harry Mead
RAMBLERS RIDING - Alan Falconer
LIFE IN THE MOORLANDS OF NORTH-EAST YORKSHIRE - Hartley + Ingilby
A WALKER ON THE CLEVELAND WAY - Colin Walker
NORTH YORK MOORS NATIONAL PARK - official C.C. guide
The National Park Authority produce a good range of publications

ORDNANCE SURVEY MAPS

These excellent maps complement the strip-maps in the guide by presenting an overall picture of the country encountered, and showing the many off-route features that might be of use or interest.

1:50,000 Landranger

sheet 93: Middlesbrough + Darlington ✳
     94: Whitby
     99: Northallerton + Ripon ✳
    100: Malton + Pickering ✳
    101: Scarborough

✳ can be dispensed with if using North York Moors 1" Tourist Map

1:25,000 maps

Outdoor Leisure 26: North York Moors, Western area
             27: North York Moors, Eastern area
Pathfinder   624: Scarborough (TA 08/09/18)

OTHER LITERATURE

CLEVELAND WAY ACCOMMODATION GUIDE (National Park)
  Free booklet listing accommodation and services

MOORS CONNECTIONS (Elmtree Publications)
  Free booklet listing all public transport in the area

Both are obtainable from the National Park Office

The Hand Stone,
Urra Moor

SOME USEFUL FACILITIES

A general guide only : includes handy off-route villages

	Youth hostel	Accommodation	Camping	Inn	Bus service	Rail service	Post Office	Other shop	payphone	WC
Helmsley	•	•		•	•		•	•	•	•
Rievaulx		•							•	•
Cold Kirby		•					•		•	
Hambleton		•		•						
Kilburn		•		•	•		•		•	
Sutton Bank								•		•
Paradise		•	•							
Osmotherley	•	•	•	•	•		•	•	•	
Huthwaite Green								•		
Swainby				•	•			•	•	
Carlton/Bank		•		•	•		•	•	•	
Cold Moor		•	•							
Clay Bank Top					•					
Great Broughton		•	•	•			•	•		
Kildale		•			•	•		•	•	•
Great Ayton		•		•	•		•	•	•	•
Guisborough		•	•		•		•	•	•	
Slapewath/Charltons		•		•	•			•		
Skelton Green		•		•	•			•		
Skelton		•	•	•	•		•	•	•	
Saltburn	•	•		•	•	•	•	•	•	•
Skinningrove					•		•	•	•	
Loftus		•		•	•		•	•	•	•
Boulby		•			•		•			
Staithes		•	•	•	•			•	•	•
Port Mulgrave		•		•	•			•		
Hinderwell		•		•	•		•	•	•	
Runswick		•		•	•		•	•	•	
Sandsend		•		•	•			•	•	•
Whitby	•	•	•	•	•	•	•	•	•	•
Robin Hood's Bay	•	•	•	•	•		•	•	•	•
Ravenscar		•	•	•	•		•	•	•	•
Cloughton		•		•	•		•	•	•	•
Scalby Mills	•	•	•	•	•			•	•	•
Scarborough		•	•	•	•	•	•	•	•	•
Cayton		•	•	•	•		•	•	•	
Gristhorpe			•	•	•		•		•	
Filey		•	•	•	•	•				•

SOME USEFUL ADDRESSES

Ramblers' Association
   1/5 Wandsworth Road, London SW8 2XX
      Tel. 071 - 582 6878

Youth Hostels Association
   Trevelyan House, St. Albans, Herts. AL1 2DY
      Tel. 0727- 55215

North York Moors National Park Information Service
   The Old Vicarage, Bondgate, Helmsley, York YO6 5BP
      Tel. 0439- 70657

Information Centres
Helmsley : Town Hall, Market Place   0439- 70173

Sutton Bank: Visitor Centre   0845 - 597426

Great Ayton: High Green   0642 - 722835

Guisborough: Fountain Street   0287- 33801

Saltburn: 4 Station Buildings, Station Square   0287- 22422

Staithes: The Old School, Staithes Lane   0947- 841251

Whitby : New Quay Road   0947- 602674

Scarborough: St. Nicholas Cliff   0723 - 373333

Filey : John Street   0723 - 512204

Bus Operators
United Automobile Services
   Grange Road, Darlington, Co.Durham DL1 5NL
      Tel. 0325- 468771

Tees and District Transport Company
   Newport Road Bus Station, Middlesbrough TS1 5AH
      Tel. 0642 - 210131

Scarborough and District Motor Services
   Valley Bridge Garage, Scarborough, N.Yorkshire
      Tel. 0723 - 375463

THE ROUTE GUIDE

The bulk of this book is a detailed guide to the walk itself, extending from page 15 to page 87. It is divided into nine daily sections, each of which has its own introduction: these can be located most easily by reference to the contents on page 5.

A continuous strip-map runs throughout the guide, accompanied by a narrative of the route on the same or facing page. The remainder of each page is then given over to notes and illustrations of the many places of interest along the way.

The maps are at the scale of 2½ inches to one mile, and the top of the page is always North.

Key to the map symbols

Route — —clear— ·—·sketchy·—· no path

Route on public road — wall — unenclosed — Fence/hedge

Abbreviations   g = gate
s = stile   c = cattle grid

Railway line

Buildings   Church   Cairns
summit other

Crags   Loose rock /scree   Marsh   Trees

river or beck → bridge — rocky shore — North Sea
steep coastal slopes and cliffs — sand and shingle

Miles from Helmsley
(73)

map continuation (indicates page number)
— — — 39

SECTION 1

─── HELMSLEY TO WHITE HORSE, KILBURN ───

9 miles (+ detour of 1?)   1125 feet of ascent

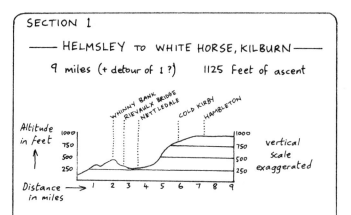

This first stage is virtually a 'breaking-in' day, which could be completed after a lunchtime start from Helmsley. There is however sufficient of interest to fill a whole day: this would then ensure the ample time recommended for appreciating Rievaulx Abbey.

Aside from that off-route saunter, the peak of the day is arrival at the Hambleton escarpment. It is in this Sutton Bank/Hambleton neighbourhood that the first of two 'official' detours takes place ~ to the White Horse of Kilburn. This excellent walk well merits the retraced steps, but by far the best solution is to break the journey at the White Horse and descend the lane to Kilburn for accommodation. The bonus is enjoying the detour on a fresh day, and seeing the Horse far better.

Helmsley

The Route

Leave Helmsley's market square by the north-western corner (nearest the church) and turn right along Church Street. Leave this by a short lane on the left bestowed with 'Cleveland Way' nameplates. It leads to a car-park, but the Way continues up a rough track. When this ends take a stile on the left, descending a field and then resume along the outside of a wood.

Beyond intervening walls a gate gives access to the wood, through which the path drops to a minor valley. Up the other side it soon leaves the trees, but remains enclosed until a lodge appears in front. Keep straight on, crossing its drive to a track heading away to the left of the lodge.

It runs above a wood before entering it and making a gradual descent onto a lane. Turn down it to shortly arrive at Rievaulx Bridge.

HELMSLEY 2½

Rievaulx

Abbey

(see page 19)

Just before reaching Rievaulx Bridge, the abbey ruins appear. This is a splendid moment.

RECOMMENDED DETOUR

River Rye

19

Abbot Hag Wood

HELMSLEY 2

Rievaulx Bridge

DETOUR: Simply turn up the lane from Rievaulx Bridge. (1 mile extra)

It is too good to miss.

We're certainly well looked-after here- on joining the lane a sign goes to the trouble to 'beware of traffic'.

Now almost hidden in undergrowth, these concrete slabs are the remains of a wartime Polish army camp.

old quarries

Quarry Bank Wood

②

Griff Lodge

463

At Rievaulx we forsake wooded Ryedale for wooded Nettledale.

Whinny Bank Wood

drive

17

Rievaulx Bridge

From the drive by the lodge a sudden and dramatic view of heavily-wooded Ryedale greets us, directly in front.

HELMSLEY to RIEVAULX BRIDGE

Helmsley is a splendid location for the start of a long-distance walk. It is a small market town set at the foot of the moors, and through it flows the River Rye. The river's final miles in the National Park take it through the grounds of adjacent Duncombe Park, former home of the Fevershams, largely rebuilt 1895.

The second earl is featured in a grand monument in the market place, where a more traditional market cross is also situated. The extensive square (which is crammed with cars 6 days a week) is lined with attractive buildings including several inns. Just around the back are the 13th century castle ruins, with the mighty keep still watching over the town. Also prominent nearby is All Saints parish church.

Helmsley also possesses a modern youth hostel, and is the National Park's administrative centre.

The castle keep

Like many in the district, the modern plantation is screened by a line of rather more indigenous trees.

16 Blackdale Howl Wood

STOKESLEY 20
B1257 ←

THE START

PICKERING 13

A170

Castle

R. Rye

THIRSK A170

Helmsley

The field-gates in the vicinity of Griff Lodge incorporate a rather clever locking device.

The only feature of interest in the first mile is the retrospective view of the castle keep. This finally disappears just before entering Blackdale Howl Wood.

The detour is the highlight

The Route

Cross straight over Rievaulx Bridge and on to a fork: keep left, and when the lane swings into a wood take a gate on the right. A wide track leads along the edge of the wood at the end of which a footbridge takes us over the beck on the right and back into a wood. Take the left-hand path to rejoin a forestry track, again at the wood's edge.

At a junction turn left up Flassendale and soon a narrow path branches right to climb out of the trees. It rises into the open, becoming a wide track soon to be enclosed as Low Field Lane to rise very gradually towards Cold Kirby. With the village in sight, a path descends right to struggle up through nettles into the village.

Head straight up the road, and after the last house on the left (just before a junction) take a track running alongside it.

The undistinguished entry into Cold Kirby has clearly been avoided by many walkers, who have chosen to remain on Low Field Lane to its terminus, there joining another lane to enter the village by the church.

Cold Kirby   A = to OLD BYLAND 2
              B = to SUTTON BANK 2

⑤   Low Field Lane

Flassen Dale

Pheasants in profusion

As height is gained on Low Field Lane, the moors to the north come into view. Also visible is the Bilsdale TV mast, which is to remain in sight for several more days.

St. Michael's, Cold Kirby

Cold Kirby is a tiny village, which at 800 feet up on the moor-edge has a reputation for living up to its name. Almost all of the houses stand detached and set tidily back from a dead-end lane. Beware- dogs in profusion

RIEVAULX BRIDGE to COLD KIRBY

Rievaulx Abbey

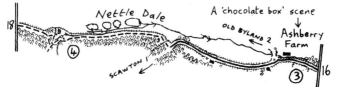

The Nettledale area is a nature reserve, the
string of ponds being a habitat of hosts of waterfowl.

Rievaulx Abbey dates from the 12th century, and it
vies with that other great Cistercian house Fountains, in the
beauty of its wooded environs: there is however a very imposing
grandeur here that is virtually unparalleled. The abbey took over
a century to build, with short canals being used to bring the
locally-quarried stone to the site.
High on the hillside above (reached by continuing up
the lane through the hamlet - note the thatched cottage) are the
exquisitely laid-out Rievaulx Terraces complete with 2 temples. Created
by the Duncombe family in the mid-18th century,
they are now maintained by the National Trust.   A nature trail

The Route

The track out of Cold Kirby is known as Cote Moor Lane, and for half a mile it forms a most pleasant green road. On emerging into a field continue to its far end and into a wood: once again our path follows its right side. At a sharp left turn take a stile in front, crossing a field to a driveway to Hambleton House on our right. Go left along it to emerge onto the Thirsk - Helmsley road, rather tidily adjacent to the Hambleton Inn.

Turn right as far as the Kilburn junction then take a path leaving the angle of the roads for the forest behind. It soon emerges into the open at the very edge of the Hambleton Hills – truly a marvellous moment. Here the Cleveland Way makes the first of its two 'official' detours, this one to visit the White Horse of Kilburn. After two miles of walking we therefore return to this point. The Horse is reached by simply turning left on the path along the rim of the drop, which swings left above Roulston Scar to arrive at the ears of the White Horse.

Having had a potter round, retrace steps back to the path junction and now continue straight on to reach the topograph above Sutton Bank. Just beyond is a fork: the right-hand path heads for the information centre, while the Way proper keeps straight on to the road.

(ROUTE EXTENDED TO SUTTON BANK TO KEEP PACE WITH MAP OPPOSITE)

The White Horse of Kilburn is a landmark of Yorkshire pride, though many have only observed it from 19 miles distant, the tower of York Minster being a popular vantage point for sharp-eyed.

This amazing creature is over 300 feet long, and was carved out of the hillside by the village schoolmaster in 1857. What sets it apart from its southern cousins is the fact that its base is not of chalk, but limestone, and consequently requires regular up-keep: visitors are begged not to walk on it. Its very size means it can only be satisfactorily seen from the vicinity of Kilburn village, the home of another famous Yorkshire 'pet'. Open to visitors are the 'Mousey' Thompson workshops, where the carved mouse climbs his furniture.

COLD KIRBY to SUTTON BANK

Sutton Bank is renowned throughout the north as 'that big hill on the way to Scarborough'. To folk from the other side of Yorkshire it forms part of the glamorous route to their coast in preference to the faster A64. Here, at Sutton Bank, is the only main road to tackle the Hambleton Hills. Its popularity is due more to its usage than any difficulties of driving. Atop it is an information centre with cafe and car-parks.

✳ Alongside the path just short of Sutton Bank is a topograph (view indicator) presented by the AA (the 'car' not 'bar' kind, that is). It records its altitude as 981 feet.

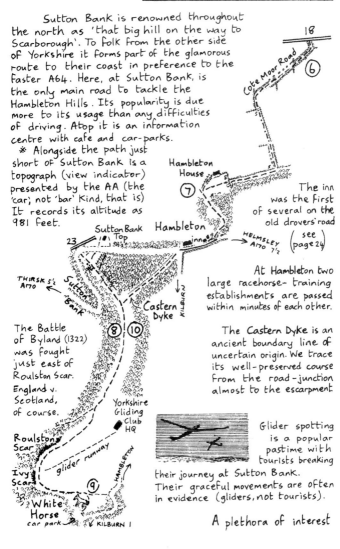

The inn was the first of several on the old drovers' road (see page 24)

At Hambleton two large racehorse-training establishments are passed within minutes of each other.

The Castern Dyke is an ancient boundary line of uncertain origin. We trace its well-preserved course from the road-junction almost to the escarpment

The Battle of Byland (1322) was fought just east of Roulston Scar. England v. Scotland, of course.

Glider spotting is a popular pastime with tourists breaking their journey at Sutton Bank. Their graceful movements are often in evidence (gliders, not tourists).

A plethora of interest

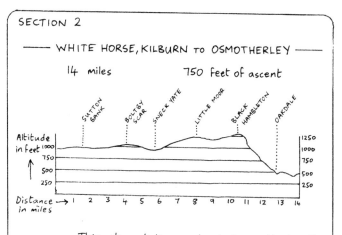

SECTION 2

—— WHITE HORSE, KILBURN TO OSMOTHERLEY ——

14 miles   750 feet of ascent

This stage takes us almost due north along the western edge of the National Park, and having gained so much height on the First section, we now take advantage of it (apart from a possible climb from Kilburn to rejoin the Way). The Hambleton Hills are trodden for almost their entire length: the edge of the steep escarpment ensures dramatic downward and extensive distant views, while the famous drove-road is a walk in the footsteps of many centuries.

Remember however that though the walking is easy en-route refreshment opportunities are scarce.

Roulston Scar and
Hood Hill from Sutton Bank

North along the Hambleton Hills from Whitestone Cliff

Gormire Lake is in view for several miles of the Way, but the sheer precipices (be warned) of Whitestone Cliff form the best viewpoint. This natural lake lies in a deep wooded hollow, with neither feeder nor outlet.

25

South Woods

Hambleton Down

1043'

Whitestone Cliff

11 A
Garbutt Wood

GOLD TYRES

21

Gormire Lake

A = Sutton Bank Nature Trail

The Hambleton escarpment at its best

The Route

The path resumes on the north side of Sutton Bank, almost at once being reinforced by the path from the car-park. From here on, the path simply clings to the edge of the escarpment. Infallible!

Looking north, note with envy the cosy setting of red-roofed Boltby village in a fold of the Hambleton Hills.

The near-neighbourhood is a renowned racehorse-training area with the Down providing ideal gallops. Indeed a racecourse once existed here at the breezy 1000 foot contour.

The Route

The path maintains its course around the huge arc containing South Woods, and at the far end rounds a gentle corner to arrive above Boltby Scar. Beyond this is a brief enclosed section avoiding a sheer drop. On re-emerging, a rare occurence is experienced - the path peters out. However we simply remain with the wall to the derelict High Barn which has long been in sight. A little beyond it, as the Sneck Yate road is neared, leave the wall on a sketchy green path which forks slightly downhill to a conspicuous gate in the wall ahead.

The road is crossed straight over and a broad track followed through a wood. At the far end it runs on to join a surfaced farm-road, which rises to High Paradise Farm and continues as a track to a T-junction. Here the Hambleton Road is at last joined, and followed left, passing through a forest before emerging on the moor at Steeple Cross.

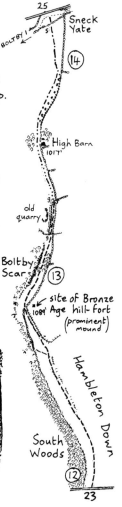

25

Sneck Yate

BOLTBY

14

High Barn
1017'

old quarry

Boltby Scar

13

site of Bronze Age hill-fort
(prominent mound)
1089'

Hambleton Down

South Woods

12

23

Boltby Scar from High Barn

A taste of Paradise

Great Whernside
is 32 miles
distant

MEUGHER 1888'

GREAT WHERNSIDE 2308'

LITTLE WHERNSIDE 1984'

BUCKDEN PIKE 2302'

PENHILL 1792'

The Yorkshire Dales skyline from Boltby Scar

26
Steeple Cross

Steeple Cross
and the Drove
Road, looking to
Black Hambleton

Boltby Forest

16
1112'
dual
carriageway

The short
section of
encroaching
forest is rendered
pleasant walking by
virtue of a 'made' path
which runs parallel to the
rough and rutted Forestry track.

Sneck Yate is the high
point of a minor road over
the Hambletons, climbing
the steep Sneck Yate Bank
to cross to Ryedale.

The Hambleton Hills take
the form of an enormous
whale-back ridge, a well-
defined western boundary of
the moors. Our route runs
virtually the entire length, initially
along the edge of the scarp, but
later on the crest of the ridge.
    This latter section from
High Paradise to Oakdale Head
takes us along the historic Hambleton
Drove Road. Though in use probably
since Bronze Age times, its fame and
magic spring from the busy droving
days centred around the 18th century.
Then it was the way of Scottish
drovers taking cattle in vast herds
to markets further south, and avoiding
in part the costly turnpike roads.

High
Paradise
(Farm)

15

High Paradise
is a real haven,
a worthy recipient
of any Cleveland Way
medal. Refreshments
on the very path
(almost literally)
in an otherwise
inhospitable
landscape are
more than
appreciated.

Sneck
Yate

HAWNBY 3

24

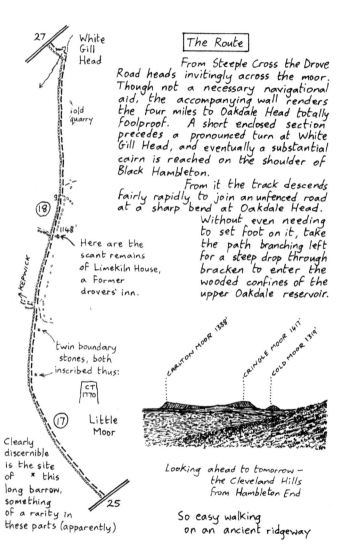

27

White Gill Head

old quarry

(18)

1148'

KEPWICK

twin boundary stones, both inscribed thus:

CT 1770

(17)

Little Moor

Clearly discernible is the site of × this long barrow, something of a rarity in these parts (apparently)

Here are the scant remains of Limekiln House, a former drovers' inn.

25

The Route

From Steeple Cross the Drove Road heads invitingly across the moor. Though not a necessary navigational aid, the accompanying wall renders the four miles to Oakdale Head totally foolproof. A short enclosed section precedes a pronounced turn at White Gill Head, and eventually a substantial cairn is reached on the shoulder of Black Hambleton.

From it the track descends fairly rapidly to join an unfenced road at a sharp bend at Oakdale Head.

Without even needing to set foot on it, take the path branching left for a steep drop through bracken to enter the wooded confines of the upper Oakdale reservoir.

CARLTON MOOR 1338'   CRINGLE MOOR 1417'   COLD MOOR 1319'

Looking ahead to tomorrow — the Cleveland Hills from Hambleton End

So easy walking on an ancient ridgeway

STEEPLE CROSS to OAKDALE

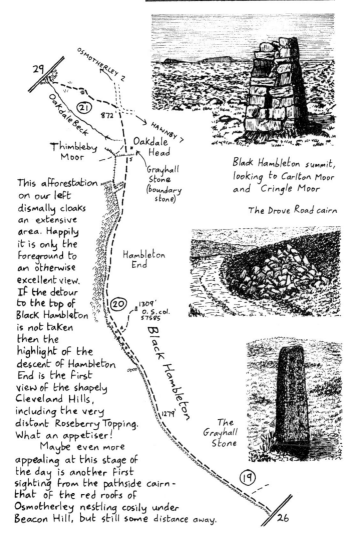

OSMOTHERLEY 2

29

Oakdale Beck

(21)

872

HAMBY 7

Thimbleby Moor

Oakdale Head

Grayhall Stone (boundary stone)

Black Hambleton summit, looking to Carlton Moor and Cringle Moor

The Drove Road cairn

This afforestation on our left dismally cloaks an extensive area. Happily it is only the foreground to an otherwise excellent view. If the detour to the top of Black Hambleton is not taken then the highlight of the descent of Hambleton End is the first view of the shapely Cleveland Hills, including the very distant Roseberry Topping. What an appetiser!

Maybe even more appealing at this stage of the day is another first sighting from the pathside cairn - that of the red roofs of Osmotherley nestling cosily under Beacon Hill, but still some distance away.

Hambleton End

(20) 1309' O.S.col. 57585

Black Hambleton

1279'

The Grayhall Stone

(19)

26

The Route

The path emerges from trees to run along the shore of Oakdale's upper reservoir. It merges into the water-board's access road, which descends to cross a sheltered corner of the lower reservoir before heading out onto a lane. A few yards to the left take a farm-track right: it is left very briefly to take a stile just beyond a gateway, then rejoined to descend to White House Farm.

Keep right of the buildings and slope down across the field, crossing a track at the bottom beyond which is a footbridge over Cod Beck. A steep climb up the wooded bank deposits us in a field with Osmotherley only two level minutes away. A couple of fields are crossed to a snicket leading onto a lane. Take the private-looking snicket opposite to emerge a novel way into the centre of the village.

Osmotherley has a highly attractive village centre which remains unaffected by the more recent housing additions. A small green marks the meeting of two roads lined by stone cottages, the main street sloping throughout its length. On the green is a sturdy market cross, adjacent to which is a stone table where Wesley once preached: just around the back is his early Methodist chapel (1754). Almost everything has a central position, with the parish church of St. Peter, with traces of Norman work, and three inns included.

Osmotherley has a 'ramblers' atmosphere', found only in certain villages; a good place from which to set forth.

OAKDALE to OSMOTHERLEY

The wooded environs of Cod Beck make for an enjoyable finish to the day. The steep climb therefrom is made easier by a worthy combination of original stone steps augmented by modern wooden ones.

Affixed to a tree at White House Farm is what would seem to be the last remaining such sign:

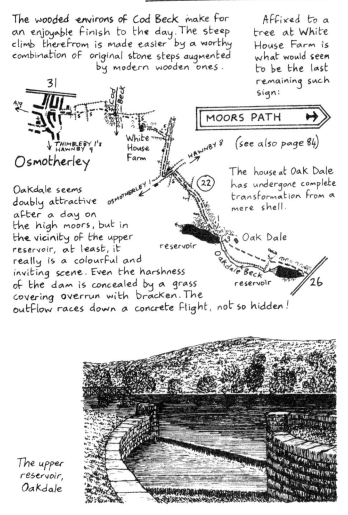

MOORS PATH →

(see also page 84)

The house at Oak Dale has undergone complete transformation from a mere shell.

Osmotherley

↓ THIMBLEBY 1½
  HAWNBY 9

Oakdale seems doubly attractive after a day on the high moors, but in the vicinity of the upper reservoir, at least, it really is a colourful and inviting scene. Even the harshness of the dam is concealed by a grass covering overrun with bracken. The outflow races down a concrete flight, not so hidden!

The upper reservoir, Oakdale

More hills than the hill-tops

SECTION 3

—— OSMOTHERLEY TO CLAY BANK TOP ——

11½ miles (+ detour of 2?)   2500 feet of ascent

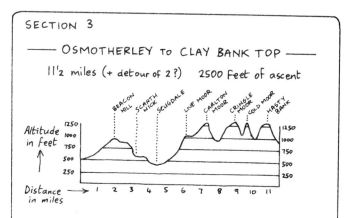

This is without a doubt the finest section of the Way, the best walk on the North York Moors and possibly the most exhilarating in the east of England. Throughout are superb views not only of the plains to north and west and the moors to south and east, but also of each of the day's hills' ever-changing aspects.

Though the miles are few and the route is obvious, it is a roller-coaster of hills. The firm recommendation is to take your time, include the early detour, and conclude with a downhill stroll into Great Broughton. Your host will probably even deposit you back on Clay Bank Top after your breakfast. Note that this is a day of 'self-sufficiency'.

Mount Grace Priory was founded in 1398, and forms the most extensive Carthusian remains in the country. As usual a beautiful setting was chosen, embowered in trees below the steep slopes of Beacon Hill. A National Trust property, it is administered by English Heritage.

Of special interest are the long rows of cells where the monks would have little difficulty in maintaining their vows of silence.

OSMOTHERLEY to BEACON HILL

The Route

        Leave the village-centre by the Swainby road climbing due north. When the houses peter out take a rough road (Rueberry Lane) to the left. This climbs a little and then heads around the hill on a level course to Chapel Wood Farm. As a field-track it remains level to enter South Wood. Take the right fork for a substantial climb to the moor-edge. A wall is followed along to the GPO station, just beyond which is the Ordnance column atop Beacon Hill (over the wall).

At the northern end of the priory grounds a gate leads into Mount Grace Wood (not a right of way, but open to bona fide priory visitors). A steep climb joins the Coast to Coast Walk to then meet the main route.

Mount Grace Priory

Mount Grace Wood

car park

Chapel Wood Farm

Rueberry Lane

SWAINBY 4

← YHA up this lune

(23)   Osmotherley

29

32

Arncliffe Wood

Beacon Hill 981'

GPO booster station

access road

South Wood

(24)

The climb to Beacon Hill is rendered a little disturbed by the constant drone of traffic on the pulsating arteries down to the left. Though this sound doesn't immediately disappear on leaving the wood, it is soon forgotten in the riot of colour which festoons the brow of the hill.

RECOMMENDED DETOUR

DETOUR:
A visit to Mount Grace Priory is well repaid, adding only a mile or so. The extended map depicts the path from Chapel Wood Farm, starting off through the farmyard. Either retrace steps, or see the note above.

A colourful departure from a colourful village

The Route

From Beacon Hill the path drops down to a corner of heather-clad Scarth Wood Moor. Opt for the track heading diagonally away to descend by a left-hand wall to the road at Scarth Nick. Cross the cattle-grid and take a gate on the right: soon the path joins a forest track. At a fork descend left to a gate. Here the Way turns sharp right to run along the bottom of the forest for a good ²/₃ mile. At a stile drop down a pathless field to cross Scugdale Beck and join a lane which is followed left to a junction at Huthwaite Green.

Leave the road here by a fenced track rising directly up towards the wood. It runs to the left before entering the wood from where a steep (and fortunately stepped) climb ensues. Happily we soon rise above the trees, and from here on the path is a wide strip rising pleasantly to the top of Live Moor.

If your visit is unfortunately not timed to coincide with the ♪ blooming heather ♫♫, console your crossing of Scarth Wood Moor with the exciting prospect of the hills ahead.

33

SWAINBY 1½

Coalmire

Scarth Wood

26

Scarth Nick

25

Scarth Wood Moor

31

OSMOTHERLEY 2

Scarth Nick is a natural pass between Beacon Hill and Whorlton Moor. Amidst a myriad of signs the following stands out:

The triangulation column on Beacon Hill is one of the Ordnance Survey's better-known structures, but its unattainable location in a field of cow-pats is a little disappointing. Here the (in)famous Lyke Wake Walk begins its march across the moors. Traditionally this is the place to gaze north-eastward with eyes bright, to that inspiring line of Cleveland Hills stretching away to the distant Roseberry Topping.

Our own route takes 64 miles to reach the same place, but at a pace to enjoy the scenery.

BEACON HILL to LIVE MOOR

Huthwaite Green is a tiny settlement which could have greatly endeared itself to passing walkers by the provision of some refreshment. This is a long stretch without such luxuries!

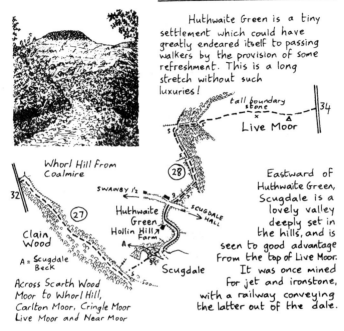

Whorl Hill from Coalmire

Clain Wood

A = Scugdale Beck

Across Scarth Wood Moor to Whorl Hill, Carlton Moor, Cringle Moor Live Moor and Near Moor

tall boundary stone
Live Moor

SWAINBY 1½

Huthwaite Green
Hollin Hill Farm

SCUGDALE HALL

Scugdale

Eastward of Huthwaite Green, Scugdale is a lovely valley deeply set in the hills, and is seen to good advantage from the top of Live Moor. It was once mined for jet and ironstone, with a railway conveying the latter out of the dale.

Ordinary woodland sandwiched between glorious moorland

34

The Route

From the top of Live Moor a modest descent is made before an equally gentle climb up to Carlton Moor alongside the glider runway. Only at the far end is it left behind to gain the Ordnance column at the moor's summit. Descent is swift: keep (firmly!) above the old alum workings directly below, to drop down to their right and soon reach the road at Carlton Bank.

Take a gate opposite, whence a level stroll precedes a pull up to the prominent memorials on Cringle End. A mild surprise awaits, as the ground continues to rise further still, in dramatic fashion past the summit of Cringle Moor before beginning to descend again.

Carlton Moor from Live Moor

Carlton 984
Carlton Bank
old alum works
Carlton Moor 1338'
O.S. column 54421

● Gliding Club HQ
(Newcastle & Teeside Gliding Club)

35

Faceby Bank
runway
runway
(30)

Running several hundred feet below the moor-tops is the well-known 'jet-miners' track', which clings to the northern slopes and passes numerous signs of former jet and alum workings.

Gold Hill
Holey Moor
white painted boundary stone

From Live Moor the track to Carlton Moor is visible all the way, with the steep western flank contrasting

33 1033' (29)
Live Moor

well with the heather carpet of the moor-top. In the fashion of its ensuing neighbours, Carlton Moor rises gently from the south to a firm top overlooking a steep fall to the Cleveland plain. This is a place to linger – select a heathery couch under the top and see how many villages can be identified with the aid of the 1" Tourist map. The nearest, appropriately is map-like Carlton.

LIVE MOOR to CRINGLE MOOR

Cringle Moor is the highest point so far achieved, and is second only to Urra Moor's Round Hill on these North York Moors. Strange then, that its summit is the only one on this escarpment which is not visited - the cairn can be seen from the path. The best feature is included however - Cringle End.

Cringle End is one of those indefinable 'good places to be'. Perched on this airy promontory are a memorial topograph and seat, and a boundary stone. Aside from the extensive views of the plain and ever-prominent Roseberry, the highlight is the dramatic plunge of Cringle's north face - real grandeur!

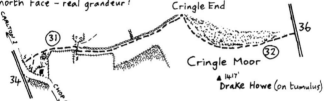

Evidence will be seen hereabouts of efforts to combat erosion on these precious hills. A sight familiar in parts of Lakeland and the Dales therefore spreads eastward again to another National Park. Here it is more closely related to the problems of the Dales, in that long-distance/challenge walks have speeded up the process.

Cringle Moor from Cringle End,
with Hasty Bank, Cold Moor and the distant Urra Moor

The Cleveland Hills at their brilliant best

ahead to
Hasty Bank

}

On
Cold Moor

}

back to
Cringle Moor

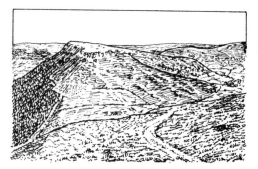

Along with ironstone and
alum, these hills were also
plundered for jet (of 'jet
black' fame), once a popular
ornamental stone. Evidence
of the mines is most apparent
when viewing Cringle Moor
from Cold Moor — just find
the right contour.

Cold Moor points a
slender finger south
towards Bilsdale, and
from its tiny cairn an
inviting path heads
away through heather.

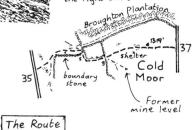

Broughton Plantation

1319'

37

shelter

Cold
Moor

35

boundary
stone

Former
mine level

The Route

The descent from Cringle Moor steepens before
a depression is reached. After following a wall away, take
a gate in it to climb easily to Cold Moor's summit. The
descent therefrom is equally rapid, and only one further
top remains.   To add even more interest, this one
possesses a new feature, the rock pinnacles of the popular
Wainstones. The path finds an easy way between the boulders,
then crosses the lengthy top of Hasty Bank.   The descent
begins steeply at the end of a cliff, dropping down to join
a forestry track at a stile. Instead of following it, the
Way continues down by the wall to emerge onto the road.

CRINGLE MOOR to CLAY BANK TOP

Cold Moor from the Wainstones

Please don't spend too long walking across Hasty Bank either a) studying the cloud formations or b) reading this. A sheer drop over a cliff may ensue which could otherwise only be achieved by following the misleading green line on a certain map

The safe descent from Hasty Bank is itself steep, but is aided by unobtrusive stone steps to combat erosion. Stretching ahead is virtually all of the next stage.

Hasty Bank is not the highest point on the Cleveland ridge, but is arguably the best. The splendid path clings to its northern edge, during which time the by-now 'commonplace' views of the Cleveland plain are supplemented by a comprehensive vista of the seemingly infinite length of Bilsdale stretching away to the south.

The Wainstones are Hasty Bank's special pride and joy, a tumbled grouping of crags and boulders guaranteed to rejuvenate even the most ancient among us— indeed, they are sufficiently aggressive to attract rock-climbers.

A switchback of superlatives

SECTION 4

—— CLAY BANK TOP TO ROSEBERRY TOPPING ——

14½ miles   1875 feet of ascent

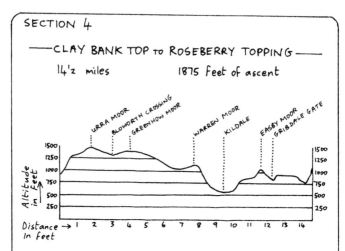

Altitude in feet

URRA MOOR
BLOWORTH CROSSING
GREENHOW MOOR
WARREN MOOR
KILDALE
EASBY MOOR
GRIBDALE GATE

1500 1250 1000 750 500 250

Distance → 1 2 3 4 5 6 7 8 9 10 11 12 13 14
in feet

This is yet another day of well-worn ways, with mile after mile of heather interspersed with tracks which encourage the traveller to really stride out. The summit of the moors is visited, and the first Captain Cook pilgrimage is made. His giant monument on Easby Moor shares a double-bill with the mini-mountain of Roseberry Topping.

The suggested halt is here, or to be more precise, Great Ayton: it is two miles distant, and a bus runs from Newton, at the foot of the Topping. The ascent of Roseberry Topping is the second of the Way's two 'official' detours, and can find itself omitted by those not seeking a bed in the neighbourhood. It's their loss!

The one supply-break occurs well into the day.

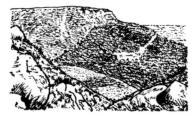

Hasty Bank
from Urra Moor

CLAY BANK TOP to ROUND HILL

The Route

Leave the road summit by taking the gate opposite, and from it a wide path rises fairly steeply at first and then very gently through the heather of Urra Moor. After a mile and a half the Ordnance column on Round Hill is reached, only a few yards left of the path.

Carlton Moor,
Cringle Moor,
Cold Moor and
Hasty Bank
From
Round Hill

The track across Urra Moor passes innumerable cairns and boundary stones.

By the path near the O.S. column is the Hand Stone, an old guidestone to 'Stoxla' (Stokesley) and 'Kirkby' (Kirkbymoorside). Its name is self-evident.

Urra Moor is the highest of the North York Moors, and not surprisingly its view is largely of rolling moorland. The summit is usually known as Round Hill, a fitting name as the pronounced mound is the site of a tumulus.

Roseberry Topping has by now been in our sights for a good few miles without seeming any nearer, but even more disconcertingly we turn our backs on it and head further away while crossing Urra Moor. For this, blame the lay-out of the Cleveland Hills, not the Way's originators. Urra Moor is also a good vantage point for appreciating the incline railway (see next page)

Urra Moor

Botton Head

Round Hill
1489'
tumulus
O.S. column
2988
A = Hand Stone

A joyous trod to the National Park summit

The old railway line we briefly follow was built in 1861 to convey ironstone from Rosedale, in the heart of the moors, to the Teesside furnaces. The sight of a train crossing the moorland at 1300 feet must have been mightily inspiring, but possibly the line's most interesting feature was the incline which lifted it onto the moor-top. A climb of 750 feet was achieved within a mile, and by a short detour we can peer straight down its course from the Incline Top. Though the line closed in 1929, this is one course that won't fade into oblivion.

On the gradual descent to Cockayne Head with layer upon layer of heather-clad moorland ahead, one can only admire Bill Cowley's noble vision so many years ago, of crossing them all to their coastal conclusion.

Burton Howe, looking north to Roseberry Topping

The inscribed stone above Greenhow Bank is a particularly fine specimen. Three sides bear directions, carved hands and the date 1757. The hollowed top suggests alms were left for the poor, a tradition still upheld as the author discovered the princely sum of 29p here on 5th Sept. 1986 (and 50p on 30th Aug. 1991).

41

Greenhow Bank

butts

guide stone

39

1405' Burton Howe

butts

site of Drum House

Incline Top

Greenhow Moor

line of former railway

Jenny Bradley (2 stones)

38

seat and stone bearing curious plaque

poor quality

butts

grouse butts

top quality

butts

37

39

Red Stone

Cockayne Head

1312'

Bloworth Crossing

Bloworth is a turning point. Where travellers once crossed the railway line, today's Cleveland Wayfarer bids farewell to the Coast-to-Coaster, leaving him to play at trains and leaving us in peace again.

ROUND HILL to WARREN MOOR

The Route

From Round Hill our track forges on, and avoiding any branches merges with an old railway track whose course can be discerned well before it is reached. Only a little further is Bloworth Crossing, a 'major' crossroads. Here the Way makes a sharp turn left. A grand track leads north for 2½ miles before a gate signals a right fork over the shoulder of Tidy Brown Hill. A gradual descent over Battersby Moor ensues to join a road, which is followed straight ahead initially on a gentle rise.

43

Warren
Juniper Moor
1099 Gate
42

BAYSDALE

41 Battersby Moor

Juniper Gate is the site of a former cross known as 'John O' Man's Cross'. This marks the high point of the moor road which leads to lonely Baysdale, once the home of a Cistercian nunnery.

Carlton Moor to Hasty Bank from Jenny Bradley

A low guide stone inscribed 'Greenhow Road' - or at least it once was.

Tidy Brown
x Hill
1300'
40
Ingleby Moor

40

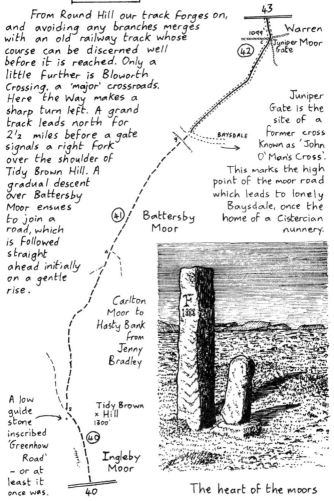

The heart of the moors

The Route

The traffic-free road descends from Warren Moor to a T-junction, and Kildale village is a mere two minutes along to the right. Just past the post-office branch off left to the railway station, leaving this lane almost immediately by a lane down to the right. It goes under the railway and climbs past Bankside Farm before a steep pull through a wood.

At the very brow of the hill a Forestry track branches left, and before long we leave that too, by a splendid path forking left. After a lengthy level stretch the path climbs right at a fork and clearing, and at a gateway a smashing surprise awaits in the shape of Cook's Monument, only yards across the heather. The last time we saw it, it was still only a distant speck.

45 / 1063
A (46)
A = Captain Cook's Monument
Easby Moor
43

The walk to Easby Moor is probably the finest woodland walk yet encountered, a level terrace with grand views over the hills of Cleveland. Even the immediate vicinity is very colourful.

Bankside Farm and the Cleveland Hills
left to right: URRA MOOR, Clay Bank Top, HASTY BANK, COLD MOOR, CRINGLE MOOR, CARLTON MOOR

Park Dyke, looking ahead to Easby Moor and Roseberry Topping

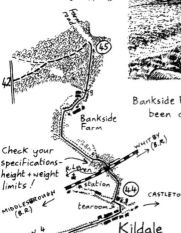

Bankside Farm is noteworthy as having been constructed in the style of the Danish 'Long House'.

Check your specifications— height + weight limits!

The railway we encounter at Kildale is rather special. One could be forgiven for thinking this rural gem survives only because the mad axeman was unaware of its existence. From Kildale the Esk Valley Line runs east to Whitby, serving nine villages in between, and meets a need in a valley where roads are narrow, steep and tortuous : it is a joy to ride — make a note. Near Kildale it reaches its summit at 560 feet, before dropping to the Cleveland plain.

Kildale is a strategically-sited village, boasting the only shop 'twixt Osmotherley and Skelton. It is the first settlement on the infant River Leven, and remains totally uncommercialised. The church of St. Cuthbert (1868) stands by the railway, near the site of the Percy Family's moated manor house.

Park Dyke is thought to be a medieval deer enclosure. With attendant wall, it remains clear.

Warren Moor

Mostly tarmac, but still very good

IN MEMORY OF
THE CELEBRATED CIRCUMNAVIGATOR
CAPT JAMES COOK F.R.S.
A MAN IN NAUTICAL KNOWLEDGE INFERIOR TO NONE,
IN ZEAL, PRUDENCE AND ENERGY SUPERIOR TO MOST.
REGARDLESS OF DANGER HE OPENED AN INTERCOURSE
WITH THE FRIENDLY ISLES AND OTHER PARTS
OF THE SOUTHERN HEMISPHERE.
HE WAS BORN AT MARTON OCT. 27TH 1728
AND MASSACRED AT OWYHEE FEB. 14TH 1779
TO THE INEXPRESSIBLE GRIEF OF HIS COUNTRYMEN.
WHILE THE ART OF NAVIGATION SHALL BE CULTIVATED
AMONG MEN, WHILE THE SPIRIT OF ENTERPRISE,
COMMERCE AND PHILANTHROPY SHALL ANIMATE
THE SONS OF BRITAIN, WHILE IT SHALL BE DEEMED
THE HONOUR OF A CHRISTIAN NATION TO SPREAD
CIVILIZATION AND THE BLESSINGS OF THE
CHRISTIAN FAITH AMONG PAGAN AND SAVAGE TRIBES,
SO LONG WILL THE NAME OF CAPT COOK
STAND OUT AMONG THE MOST CELEBRATED AND
MOST ADMIRED BENEFACTORS OF THE HUMAN RACE.

———

AS A TOKEN OF RESPECT FOR
AND ADMIRATION OF THAT GREAT MAN
THIS MONUMENT WAS ERECTED BY
ROBERT CAMPION ESQ. OF WHITBY A.D. 1827

———

BY THE PERMISSION OF THE OWNER OF THE EASBY ESTATE
J.J. EMERSON ESQ. IT WAS RESTORED IN 1895
BY THE READERS OF THE NORTH EASTERN DAILY GAZETTE

———

The tablet on Captain Cook's Monument
Easby Moor

EASBY MOOR to ROSEBERRY TOPPING

Roseberry Topping
1050'
Roseberry Common
784'
Newton Moor
995'
OS col. 54415
← severe erosion on upper slopes

※ Just through this gate the unrivalled symmetry and general grandeur of the Topping will stop you in your tracks.

(48)

← two boundary stones ※
(by chance marking the new boundary)
butts

Great Ayton Moor
site of Iron age field enclosure

※ Cleveland county is here entered

(47)

Roseberry Topping is Cleveland's Matterhorn, and try telling the good people under its shadow (or should that be its spell?) that it's not a real mountain. The unique profile and position certainly belie its modest stature, the profile having been further 'enhanced' by the dramatic rock-face immediately west of the summit, a result of a landfall due to earlier mining. The airy top is solid rock, and the view solid gold. Great Ayton and Newton-under-Roseberry appear in true birds-eye fashion: a stretch of coastline is also visible. Roseberry and its Common recently fell into the safe hands of the National Trust.

The Route

Several paths radiate from the Monument, but the broad way heading north is clearly ours. It descends through afforestation (not a nice word but not a nice meaning) to a car-park at Gribdale Gate.

Go right a few yards then take the path climbing steeply opposite. At the top a grand level walk along the moor-edge follows. Eventually a gate is reached, and through it Roseberry Topping re-appears across the depression of Roseberry Common. The path is unmistakeable: go for it!

GREAT AYTON
750' Gribdale Gate

Easby Moor 1064'
42

Gribdale Gate is a natural gap between moors. Here the Forestry Commission has provided a car-park (big deal) which explains the crowds flocking to Cook's Monument who otherwise would most likely never have reached it.

Two famous landmarks linked

SECTION 5

— ROSEBERRY TOPPING TO SALTBURN —

10 miles   900 feet of ascent

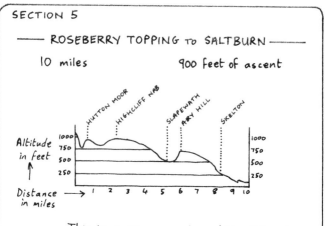

This is a very easy day, which will have been added to by a restart from Great Ayton. After a farewell to the moors a complete contrast is experienced in a long march through Guisborough Woods. Beyond, civilisation is encountered in a down-to-earth way, and Saltburn beckons us the last varied miles.

Arrival at the coast is an exciting event, and this day of all the days on the Cleveland Way is the one with least chance of plummeting over a cliff-face.

Roseberry Topping from Newton-under-Roseberry

ROSEBERRY TOPPING to HUTTON MOOR

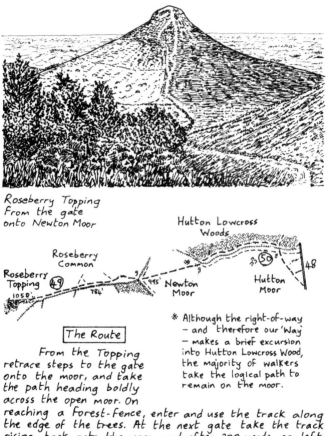

Roseberry Topping
from the gate
onto Newton Moor

The Route

From the Topping
retrace steps to the gate
onto the moor, and take
the path heading boldly
across the open moor. On
reaching a forest-fence, enter and use the track along
the edge of the trees. At the next gate take the track
rising back onto the moor, and after 200 yards go left
on a narrow level branch. Here again, walkers have forged
a more direct way just above the forest boundary.

✻ Although the right-of-way
— and therefore our 'Way'
— makes a brief excursion
into Hutton Lowcross Wood,
the majority of walkers
take the logical path to
remain on the moor.

Farewell to the Matterhorn

The Route

The level path across the moor soon drops down to merge with the unofficial path at a wall-corner. From here it follows the wall uphill as far as a gate into a corner of Guisborough Woods. A good path heads through the trees, crossing a forestry track before arriving at Highcliff Nab, an oasis in the trees. The path climbs up behind the rock and soon joins forces with a level forestry track. At a fork descend to the left, then another level stretch comes to a T-junction on a sharp bend. Opt for the short climb right, just beyond which a left fork maintains our level course.

A staggered crossroads forms the next junction: keep straight on to a T-junction, where a left turn leads almost immediately out of the wood. The track runs with a field now on its right. Look for a stile on the right to sketchily cross a level field to join a concrete drive. This is followed down to the edge of the trees, where a narrow enclosed path takes us off to the right.

Highcliff Nab, looking beyond Guisborough to the coast

Just beyond the Nab, a break in the trees above a line of heather-capped crags provides a colourful scene with distant views.

Highcliff Nab

1000'

Highcliffe Farm

49

51

47

On entering the woods bid a last farewell to the heather moors which have kept us company since Sutton Bank. Be ye not despondent however, for in sight ahead (admittedly only intermittently at the moment thanks to the odd tree) is the coast, which marks the onset of the second half of this great walk. And you will not be disappointed.

HUTTON MOOR to SLAPEWATH

Highcliff Nab is a substantial rock-face protruding from the near-blanket covering of Guisborough Woods. It serves as an excellent viewpoint in a section where distant views are thin on the ground. Laid out map-like below is Guisborough itself: hardly spectacular but nevertheless quite a sight. Keen eyes will pick out the lofty feature of the Priory arch, locked in its town-centre location by a solid ring of modern housing.   The Nab is also of use to rock-climbers.

On leaving Highcliff Nab we also leave the 1000-foot contour for the last time.

Spa Wood 50

Guisborough Woods

53

52

48

By this clearing we have finally passed Guisborough. To the right of the town is the conspicuous Guisborough Hall.

The long march through the forest is not the trial that might have been anticipated. The tracks are everywhere clear and pleasant. Navigation is further aided by waymarked rocks at junctions.

Fox and Hounds, Slapewath

Hardly a classic hostelry, but it *is* the first on the route since Osmotherley.

The end of the moors couldn't be better **defined**

The Route

Enclosed by fences our path arrives at a stile on the left: do not use it but turn sharp right. With woods to the right and a part-reclaimed quarry to the left, remain on this level path to a T-junction with a wide track. Turn down it to join a road. Go left along this short section left in peace by road-widening, and when it expires cross the parallel main road. A few paces further escape down to the inn at Slapewath.

Briefly on the old road again, leave it by a path after the row of houses just past the inn. It climbs steeply to the right of an old quarry and round its rim. An overgrown enclosed path leads to a field from where a rise to the right becomes a track to Airy Hill Farm. Remain on it, now as the farm's access road leading unerringly down to Skelton Green.

At the road-corner go straight on to the main road and across that to a wicket-gate. A tarmac footway heads through the fields to drop to a lane: steps in front lead down into the centre of Skelton. continued opposite

51

SKELTON

A = inns

Fish + chips!

Skelton Green

BOOSBECK

stables 'Manless Terrace'

56

Airy Hill Lane

Airy Hill Lane is astride a modest ridge, providing a wide prospect of the sea and villages in between. Down to the right is Boosbeck, while ahead and to the right is larger Brotton.

mast × 718'

Airy Hill Farm

55

While Skelton Green has remained small, Skelton has emerged as big brother, with much new housing. Of most interest however is Skelton Castle, an enormous house on the Guisborough road. Dating from 1794, it remains in private hands. It is on the site of a 12th century castle. Adjacent is a redundant old church.

Former alum quarry

overgrown old road

GUISBOROUGH A171 2¼

'former' tip

54

Spa Wood

Slapewath

WHITBY 20 A171

Charltons

National Park vacated

Slapewath is a bizarre place, a gap in the hills once exploited by a railway line and alum and ironstone miners.

49

This is Saltburn's Sunday name, which gets as much of an airing on Sundays as it does any other day.

Route-note: If passing straight through Saltburn, pathways through the Valley Gardens will lead all the way to the seafront.

A = Riftswood Viaduct a near 800'-long red brick structure

Skelton's street-names conjure up visions of far more exotic places!

Saltburn by-the-Sea

pier

station

MIDDLESBROUGH (B.R.) ←

MARSKE 2½ A174

53

Valley Gardens

miniature railway

59

Skelton Beck

58

mineral line

(see page 54)

Civic Hall

GUISBOROUGH 3

57

BROTTON 2 A173

Skelton

50

Route continued

Cross Skelton's main street and then negotiate some modern housing by way of Coniston Road, Ullswater Drive and Derwent Road before escaping into a field. A good path then crosses several fields to enter woods. After an early fork right the path descends to a footbridge over Skelton Beck and under a viaduct. A little below it take an enclosed track up left— the youth hostel is just at the top— but if heading straight for the front leave the track at a sharp bend left, by branching right. A good path through the woods (avoiding deviations) joins a drive up onto the road in Saltburn. For the seafront, just keep right.

Riftswood Viaduct, Skelton Beck

A varied approach to the coast

SECTION 6

——— SALTBURN TO RUNSWICK ———

12½ miles   1425 feet of ascent

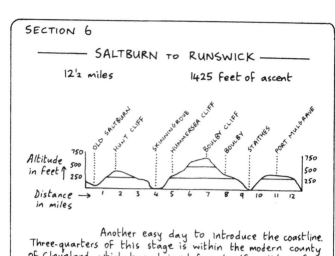

Altitude in feet ↑

Distance in miles →

        Another easy day to introduce the coastline.
Three-quarters of this stage is within the modern county
of Cleveland, which has claimed for itself, with a fair
degree of justification, two of the most impressive cliffs:
one of these is the highest in the country. Twice we sink
to sea-level, but the occasions could not contrast more.
Both are old fishing ports but for reasons which become
clear only one draws the tourists. Staithes is another
stop on the trail of Captain Cook, and this is the place
to use up any spare time.

Old Saltburn
and Hunt Cliff

SALTBURN to HUNT CLIFF

Saltburn is our first taste of the seaside, and it provides a good example of the individuality which will be found amongst the coastal towns and villages. Until the mid-19th century Saltburn was a small fishing village, but then the railway from Middlesbrough was extended here, and thus a holiday resort was created. The town stands high above the seaward slopes, facing the attractively-wooded Valley Gardens rather than the sea.

At sea-level is Old Saltburn, consisting chiefly of an inn, the boat-landings and a former mortuary the size of a garden hut. The extended inn is renowned as a haunt of smugglers in days gone by. Beyond it the cliffs begin in earnest, and Hunt Cliff forms a striking headland.

Today Saltburn still has its railway and its spread of Victorian residences, but it also seems to have an air of unfashionableness. One claim to fame it can make however, is the possession of the last surviving pleasure pier on the old Yorkshire coast.

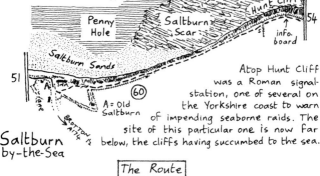

Atop Hunt Cliff was a Roman signal-station, one of several on the Yorkshire coast to warn of impending seaborne raids. The site of this particular one is now far below, the cliffs having succumbed to the sea.

Saltburn by-the-Sea

The Route

From the main road above the Valley Gardens a zigzag road descends to the front (steps can be used to cheat the bends). Turn right to the Ship Inn, and only a few yards up the road behind, two paths set off up the steep slopes. The newer, left-hand one is most direct, while the gentler right-hand one runs to a row of cottages before doubling back to the top of the cliffs. The cliff path now rises gently to Hunt Cliff.

An inspiring introduction to cliff-land

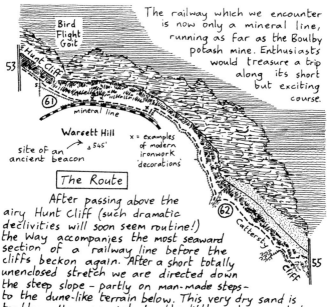

The railway which we encounter is now only a mineral line, running as far as the Boulby potash mine. Enthusiasts would treasure a trip along its short but exciting course.

Bird Flight Goit

53

Hunt Cliff

61

mineral line

Warsett Hill △ 545'

site of an ancient beacon

x = examples of modern ironwork 'decorations'

62

Cattersty Cliff

55

The Route

After passing above the airy Hunt Cliff (such dramatic declivities will soon seem routine!) the Way accompanies the most seaward section of a railway line before the cliffs beckon again. After a short totally unenclosed stretch we are directed down the steep slope – partly on man-made steps – to the dune-like terrain below. This very dry sand is trodden rather ungainly to the little underpass below Skinningrove's jetty. Beyond it a rough path leads directly to the village itself.

A short stroll along the road leads across the bridge over Kilton Beck. As the road begins to climb we forsake it for a steeper climb back to the cliff-tops. A three-quarter mile walk atop Hummersea Cliff precedes a detour inland by way of a fenced path. This joins a cart-track near Hummersea Farm, which is followed away to the left.

On Hunt Cliff

HUNT CLIFF to HUMMERSEA

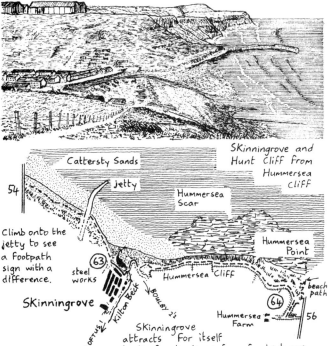

SKinningrove and Hunt Cliff from Hummersea Cliff

Cattersty Sands

jetty

Hummersea Scar

54

Hummersea Point

Climb onto the jetty to see a footpath sign with a difference.

steel works

Hummersea Cliff

beach path

SKinningrove

Kilton Beck

BOULBY 2½

LOFTUS 1

Hummersea Farm

64

56

SKinningrove attracts for itself a host of adjectives, few of which are complimentary: remarkable, however, it certainly is. Our stroll along dramatic cliffs is disrupted well before reaching the village, as we descend old slag-heaps to the beach. Once an innocent little fishing port, things changed in the mid-19th century when a particularly good seam of ironstone was discovered: the village is still dominated by the modern steelworks on the hill-top.

The foreshore is littered with debris and a warning sign about eating seafood is superfluous, particularly on seeing the colour of the beck. The pigeons must be happy enough, their lofts far outnumbering the houses.

Far from the madding crowd

The old alum workings on Boulby Cliff, looking to Staithes

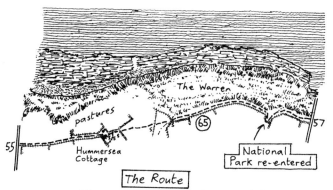

The Route

       The cart-track ends at an isolated house, but stiles straight ahead lead to a narrow path rising through thick bracken. On climbing a field beyond, the cliff-top is regained, and the way remains clear to shortly surmount the high cliffs of Boulby. After passing an information board and up to the right an Ordnance column, a gradual descent commences through an extensive area of bracken. Rockhole Hill is rounded before a short steep descent by a wall precedes a level walk to the cottages of Boulby. Just keep straight on, avoiding any deviations.

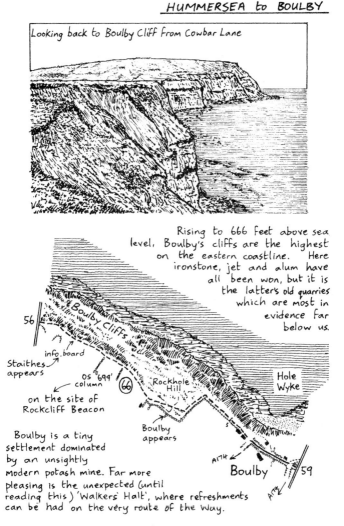

Looking back to Boulby Cliff from Cowbar Lane

Rising to 666 feet above sea level, Boulby's cliffs are the highest on the eastern coastline. Here ironstone, jet and alum have all been won, but it is the latters' old quarries which are most in evidence far below us.

Boulby Cliffs

56

info. board

Staithes appears

OS '699' column ⑥⑥ Rockhole Hill

on the site of Rockcliff Beacon

Hole Wyke

Boulby appears

A174

Boulby 59

A174

Boulby is a tiny settlement dominated by an unsightly modern potash mine. Far more pleasing is the unexpected (until reading this) 'Walkers' Halt', where refreshments can be had on the very route of the Way.

A climb to the highest cliff

BOULBY to STAITHES

Staithes is a fishing port and a former smuggling centre, and despite tourism it remains a delightful place. A large portion stands up by the Whitby - Middlesbrough road, but the crowd-puller is the lower half by the seafront. Here many buildings cluster into little space, either perched above the deep-cut beck or facing the small harbour. It is the sea that is linked with every aspect of Staithes life. The boats sheltering in the mouth of the beck will be seen, and the Mission Church of St. Peter the Fisherman. Staithes has its share of savage storms, and the seafront Cod and Lobster inn has often been a prime target.

Here James Cook earned his first wages serving in a shop, and a story relates how a south-sea coin he took in inspired him to go forth on his life of adventure. The beck now forms the county boundary, and the north bank, known as Cowbar, marks our last steps in Cleveland county.

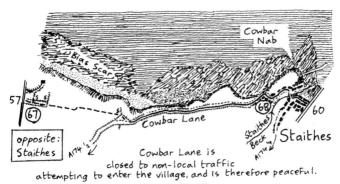

Cowbar Lane is closed to non-local traffic attempting to enter the village, and is therefore peaceful.

The Route

At the second lane to leave Boulby for the main road, the Way continues straight on through fields to join Cowbar Lane near the cliff-tops. This quiet road conveys us into Staithes, ultimately in dramatic fashion. It descends into the heart of the village, where a footbridge is crossed to join the main street before heading left to arrive at the seafront.

A simple walk into a spectacular setting

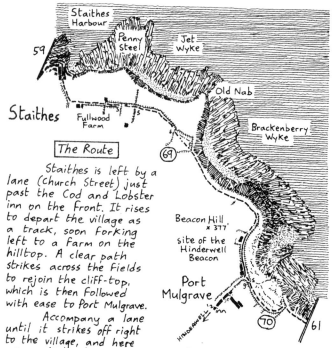

Staithes Harbour
59
Penny Steel
Jet Wyke
Old Nab
Brackenberry Wyke
Staithes
Fullwood Farm
69
Beacon Hill × 377'
site of the Hinderwell Beacon
Port Mulgrave
HINDERWELL inn
70 61

The Route

Staithes is left by a lane (Church Street) just past the Cod and Lobster inn on the front. It rises to depart the village as a track, soon forking left to a farm on the hilltop. A clear path strikes across the fields to rejoin the cliff-top, which is then followed with ease to Port Mulgrave.

Accompany a lane until it strikes off right to the village, and here we continue to contour around the tiny harbour far below. The cliff-top is followed for a further short mile before turning inland at a pond to enter Runswick Bank Top. Its partner Runswick Bay is just down that steep road leaving the junction on which we've emerged.

Port Mulgrave is a homely place known chiefly for its mini-harbour. At one stage visible from our route high above, it was constructed in the mid-19th century when the mining of iron-ore was in full swing. The ore was brought through a mile-long tunnel (the closed-off entrance still adorns the cliff) before being shipped up the coast to large ironworks.

Sadly the scene today is of near-dereliction, with the short harbour walls well past their best. Half a dozen or so local boats still manage to make use of the shelter. Note the long terrace of former miners' cottages just inland of our route. A little further inland is Hinderwell, a larger village on the A174.

STAITHES to RUNSWICK

Looking to Kettle Ness from Port Mulgrave

Runswick is a village of contrasts: while Runswick Bank Top is plain, its lower half of Runswick Bay is a dazzling grouping of bright cottages in total disarray in the shadow of the cliff. This delectable corner boasts an enviable position, facing south across its own bay.

A labyrinth of paths wind in between the numerous dwellings. Once fishermen's homes, many are now used only as holiday homes.

Rosedale Wyke

60

A sign at the pond warns of it being a habitat of the Great Crested Newt. Better a wide berth than a savage mauling.

Lingrow Cliffs

pond

71

Runswick Bank Top

HINDERWELL

WHITBY

Runswick Bay

RUNSWICK BAY

63

From one 'classic' village to another

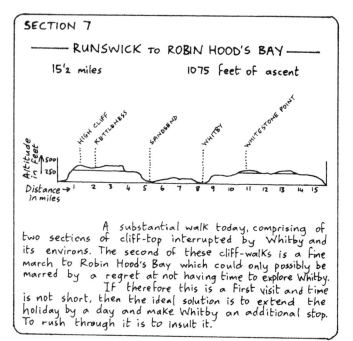

SECTION 7

—— RUNSWICK TO ROBIN HOOD'S BAY ——

15½ miles   1075 feet of ascent

A substantial walk today, comprising of two sections of cliff-top interrupted by Whitby and its environs. The second of these cliff-walks is a fine march to Robin Hood's Bay which could only possibly be marred by a regret at not having time to explore Whitby.

If therefore this is a first visit and time is not short, then the ideal solution is to extend the holiday by a day and make Whitby an additional stop. To rush through it is to insult it.

Whitby Abbey

RUNSWICK to KETTLENESS

Runswick Bay
From Hob Holes

The Route

The steep road down to Runswick Bay terminates adjacent to the village in a surround of car-parks. A short promenade leads us onto the beach, and the sands are trodden for half a mile to the first deep rift in the newly-reformed cliffs. This initially dubious-looking exit is in fact simple: a footbridge over the beck precedes a steep climb to the cliff-top. The way is then straightforward, with only a brief diversion from the cliffs to pass around the Kettleness farm buildings.

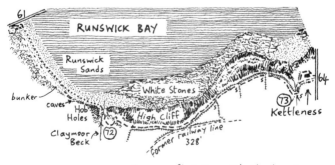

A rare flirtation with the beach

The old railway
tunnel entrance,
Kettleness

Rounding Kettle
Ness is an inspiring
moment as Whitby
appears as the next
headland but one: the
piers, BBC mast and the
dark shadow of the abbey (not
on the skyline) may be located.

Kettleness is a tiny community that
was once larger. For more than a century
and a half ago a previous hamlet fell victim to the sea.
This was also the site of another Roman signal station,
while more recently alum was quarried extensively on the
prominent nab reaching out to Kettle Ness itself.

Kettle Ness from High Cliff

KETTLENESS to SANDSEND

The Route

On passing between the farm buildings at Kettleness a lane-head is reached. Here branch left on a path to regain the cliff-tops above the point of Kettle Ness. The Way soon rises a little sketchily past an old tunnel entrance to the high point of Seaveybog Hill. A short mile further an intervening wall points the way of a short-cut to avoid circumnavigating a field before being confronted by a surprisingly steep descent through trees.

This proves a real test for knees, but amends are soon made by the fact that there isn't a corresponding re-ascent on this occasion. At the bottom, hidden in foliage is the southern entrance to the old railway tunnel, and from it the old track-bed is followed gradient-free towards Sandsend. Just before getting there the old railway station appears ahead, and just prior to it the Way forks left to descend steps into a car-park. At its entrance the road is joined and is followed along Sandsend's front.

64

Overdale Wyke

tunnel entrance

Deepgrove Wyke

Sandsend Ness

old quarries

76

National Park vacated

LYTHE, A174

Sandsend

66

After a brief flirtation with the former Rosedale railway at Bloworth Crossing (remember that far back?) here is a longer chance to chug along. What a journey this must have been, through the Yorkshire coast resorts, always near the cliffs and at times hugging them.

Having rounded Sandsend Ness the village appears ahead, and perhaps more excitingly, Whitby is now at the end of the bay.

A must for old railway fans

The Route

With a footway almost all the way the road leads us through Sandsend towards Whitby, being deflected away from the sea by a golf course. A little past a side-road to Newholm take an enclosed track to the left, descending below a high footbridge to reach the terminus of a newly constructed promenade. We are now presented with a bewildering range of options. Up to the right a path meets a road and generally follows the crest of the cliff; a path traverses between there and the 'prom'; the prom itself awaits; as does the beach, if the tide is out.

Arrival at Captain Cooks statue is a fine moment, with all spread below. Descend the path under the whale-bone arch onto a winding road (the Khyber Pass) which descends to and runs by the outer harbour.

Sandsend's name should raise few queries, for here the long stretch of sandy beach from Whitby comes to an abrupt halt as the rocky shoreline takes over. This is worth noting as, tide permitting, here is a rare opportunity to stroll along a good beach, a worthwhile escape from the road walk towards Whitby.

Sandsend was a major centre of the alum industry, and on approaching the village we pass through what once was an area of extensive quarrying. Looking back to Sandsend Ness we can see the result of the quarrying which actually substantially changed the appearance of the headland. Another change of appearance occurred only in the 1960's, when the closure of the exhilarating coastal railway resulted in the demolition of the viaducts: a little evidence remains.

Strictly speaking, Sandsend is two tiny villages, with East Row forming one half. Each stands at the foot of its own beck (which run parallel), and as each is crossed we can look inland to equally charming scenes of beckside cottages and woods.

SANDSEND to WHITBY

Whitby is, in the author's humblest of opinions, the finest coastal town in the land. The old saying 'familiarity breeds contempt' goes out of the window here: to tire of Whitby would be to tire of most things.

The town's position of near-isolation at the edge of the moors has enabled it to retain much of its identity and it is the sea where Whitby's allegiance lies. Curiously enough though the town does not face up to the sea, but instead straddles the last mile of the River Esk which, once again curiously, enters the North Sea by flowing due north. The result of this is a rare opportunity, if lucky, to see the sun rise and set over the North Sea.

Whitby is steeped in history, and its great names are recalled in their own particular ways. The founder of the abbey, St. Hilda, has the dedication of the parish church in the town-centre; while Caedmon, father of the English hymn, is remembered by a 20-feet memorial cross outside St. Mary's church on the East Cliff. Meanwhile the West Cliff boasts a whalebone arch, a souvenir of the days when whalers set off from here Arctic-bound, including the most successful of his time, William Scoresby; only a few yards distant is a statue of Captain James Cook, gazing evocatively over the harbour-mouth from where this celebrated explorer set sail on his epic voyages of adventure.

continued overleaf

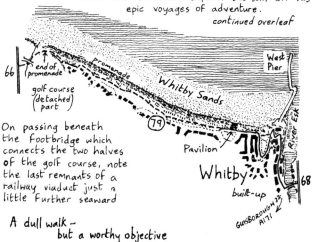

66

end of promenade

golf course (detached) part)

Promenade

Whitby Sands

West Pier

79

Pavilion

Whitby

built-up

River Esk

68

GUISBOROUGH 23, A171

On passing beneath the footbridge which connects the two halves of the golf course, note the last remnants of a railway viaduct just a little further seaward

A dull walk — but a worthy objective

Saltwick Nab was the scene of a famous shipwreck drama in 1914, when the 'Rohilla' a hospital ship bound for Dunkirk, ran aground. Whitby's museum chronicles the stirring rescue.

East Pier

River Esk

YH

80

Abbey

Abbey Farm

HAWSKER 2½

National Park re-entered

81

Whitby

67

Saltwick Nab

North Batts

Saltwick Bay

holiday village (shop, phone)

ROAD (private)

69

Between Abbey Farm and the cliffs is the Coastguard operation room and also a BBC mast.

Whitby - continued from previous page

A swing-bridge links Whitby's two halves and also its two harbours, which are centred on the west bank of the Esk. In the outer harbour is the fish quay where one can watch the landing and the buying and selling, inhale the smell and generally take in the atmosphere of it all. Further sea-going connections include an important shipbuilding history and a striking building on the east bank, the seamen's almshouses.

Between the fish quay and the west pier is Whitby's modest amusement quarter, and also on this side of the river are the bulk of the shops and the Pannett Park museum, with a splendid display of local interest. Here too is the railway station, terminus of the Esk valley line.

East of the river the houses and shops huddle tightly under the cliff. In their midst are a popular glass-blowing establishment, a tempting fudge-making shop and a traditionally-cured kipper merchant. Climbing up to the cliff-top are the 199 steps alongside which is the cobbled and equally-steep 'Donkey Road'. At the top are the windswept gravestones of St. Mary's parish church, a squat, solid structure dating from the 12th century: the interior has a fascinating layout. In a similarly-exposed situation alongside are the abbey ruins. The original abbey dated from 657, and within its first decade it hosted the synod that decided the setting of the feast of Easter.

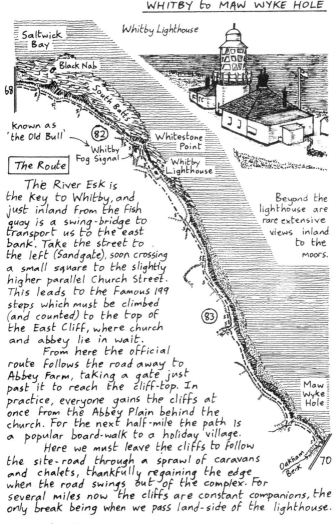

Saltwick Bay

Black Nab

68

South Batts

Whitby Lighthouse

known as
'the Old Bull'

(82)
Whitby
Fog Signal

Whitestone
Point

Whitby
Lighthouse

Beyond the
lighthouse are
rare extensive
views inland
to the
moors.

(83)

Maw
Wyke
Hole

Oakham
Beck

70

The Route

   The River Esk is
the key to Whitby, and
just inland from the fish
quay is a swing-bridge to
transport us to the east
bank. Take the street to
the left (Sandgate), soon crossing
a small square to the slightly
higher parallel Church Street.
This leads to the famous 199
steps which must be climbed
(and counted) to the top of
the East Cliff, where church
and abbey lie in wait.
   From here the official
route follows the road away to
Abbey Farm, taking a gate just
past it to reach the cliff-top. In
practice, everyone gains the cliffs at
once from the Abbey Plain behind the
church. For the next half-mile the path is
a popular board-walk to a holiday village.
   Here we must leave the cliffs to follow
the site-road through a sprawl of caravans
and chalets, thankfully regaining the edge
when the road swings out of the complex. For
several miles now the cliffs are constant companions, the
only break being when we pass land-side of the lighthouse.

A return to tranquillity - in stages

69

84

At Maw Wyke Hole Wainwright's Coast to Coast Walk reaches its goal of the east coast, after 187 miles walking from St Bees on the Cumbrian coast. It now accompanies the Cleveland Way for its last three miles to the sea at Robin Hood's Bay.

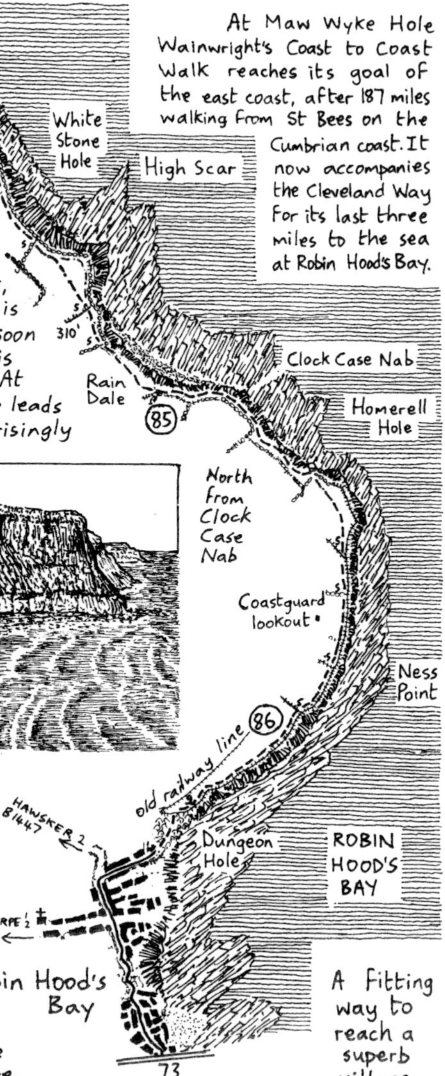

White Stone Hole

High Scar

The Route

On eventually rounding Ness Point, Robin Hood's Bay is fully in view, and soon the village itself is within our sights. At last a wicket-gate leads into trees to surprisingly

310'

Rain Dale

85

Clock Case Nab

Homerell Hole

North from Clock Case Nab

Coastguard lookout

Ness Point

86

old railway line

emerge onto a street, Mount Pleasant North. From the road at the far end turn left to descend the busy main street all the way down through the village centre to the stony shore.

HAWSKER B1447 2

FYLINGTHORPE ½ A171

Dungeon Hole

ROBIN HOOD'S BAY

Robin Hood's Bay

73

A fitting way to reach a superb village

MAW WYKE HOLE to ROBIN HOOD'S BAY

Robin Hood's Bay, with the advantages of an exciting name and an even more exciting location, will be found in many people's list of favourite places. Known in the locality as just Bay Town, it consists of a chaotic tumble of red-roofed buildings squeezed into only a narrow gap between cliffs. From the modern extension to the village where we join it at the cliff-top, the steep main street plunges down to the very shore. On each side are irregular groupings of shops and dwellings, with short and narrow passageways linking the near-hidden doorsteps.

The village has suffered badly from storms in times past, and the Bay Hotel on the seafront once had a ship driven into it by the savage weather. A modern sea-wall now ensures a little more safety. Near the top of the main street is a plaque commemorating an incredible sea rescue of 1881, which involved hauling a lifeboat six miles overland, through snow, in order to be launched.

The bay itself is also full of interest, and is generally regarded as a geologist's mecca, with fossils in abundance and a spectacular sweep of flat scars which curve round the bay almost as a natural extension of the tide. Throughout most of the walk from the village up to Ravenscar this can be well appreciated at low tide.

The story behind the name is that our hero in Lincoln green journeyed here fairly regularly to relax in peace far from his enemies. It is said he had boats at the ready if a need arose to flee the land. Whatever the reality, it's still a good name!

Definitely once the preserve of fishermen and smugglers, the village is now very much a part of the tourist's itinerary.

SECTION 8

── ROBIN HOOD'S BAY TO SCARBOROUGH ──

15 miles   1300 feet of ascent

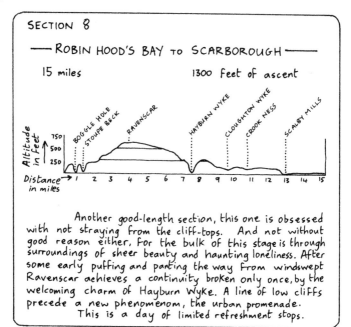

Altitude in feet / Distance in miles

BOGGLE HOLE / STOUPE BECK / RAVENSCAR / HAYBURN WYKE / CLOUGHTON WYKE / CROOK NESS / SCALBY MILLS

        Another good-length section, this one is obsessed with not straying from the cliff-tops.   And not without good reason either, for the bulk of this stage is through surroundings of sheer beauty and haunting loneliness. After some early puffing and panting the way from windswept Ravenscar achieves a continuity broken only once, by the welcoming charm of Hayburn Wyke. A line of low cliffs precede a new phenomenom, the urban promenade.
        This is a day of limited refreshment stops.

Boggle
Hole
Youth
Hostel

ROBIN HOOD'S BAY to RAVENSCAR

The Route

Departure from Robin Hood's Bay is very well-defined. Take a tiny lane (Albion Street) virtually at the very foot of the main street, to climb stone steps to the cliffs where more recently-made steps take over. Two deep wooded valleys soon hamper progress by causing returns to sea-level. The first shelters the youth hostel at Boggle Hole: both at least provide footbridges.

From the second of these, concrete paving-stones climb to Stoupe Bank Farm. Its lane is followed until just past a dip and a bend, where a stile then returns us to the cliff-top.

With the lofty heights of Ravenscar's cliffs ahead, the path remains on these lower cliffs for some time, passing above Miller's Nab where the original path vacated the cliffs at an earlier stage.

The paving-stones above Stoupe Beck may appear rather incongruous but their practical value far exceeds their lack of aesthetic value. And what a gradient!

Standing at the foot of the deep-cut valley of Mill Beck, Boggle Hole Youth Hostel is not seen until its front gate is reached. The building was originally a mill, and must now rank as one of the most spectacularly-sited hostels in the country.

The coastline's answer to the Cleveland Hills

Low Nook

Old Peak

73

The Coomb

Peak
Alum Trail

golf course
in an enviable
setting

Hotel

National
Trust centre

The pull
up to Ravenscar
can justifiably
be punctuated
by halts to
take in the
fine view back
across Robin
Hood's Bay.

90

625

Ravenscar

PO

Station Road

path to
bunkbarn
and tearooms

91

Blea
Wyke

75

Here at
Ravenscar
the Way
makes its
only real
break from
the coast,
and this
but a
brief
one.

Ravenscar is unlike any of the
other coastal towns and villages. For a start
it is perched at a breezy 600ft. up on the
cliff-tops, and for this very reason it failed
dismally as a planned holiday venue even before
it started. In the 1890s work began on establishing a resort,
but the location proved to be too off-putting for too many
folk, and the idea was abandoned after thirty years. Some
signs of the intended street lay-out are still in evidence.

On a sunny day however this is a wonderful
place to be, rich in nature, geology and bracing sea air. A
geological trail has been created, and a leisurely exploration
of the extensive undercliff is most rewarding for those with
time. Of further interest are a National Trust information
centre, bunk-barn facilities, old alum quarries and the end
of the Lyke Wake Massacre. Please step gently over any
survivors. The former railway line now serves as a splendid
footpath, if not quite up to the standard of our impending
cliff path.

On one of the afore-mentioned days of good
weather, Flamborough Head may just be discerned far
down the coastline. This is something of a psychological
boost, for we know that our objective of Filey Brigg is on
this side of it, somewhere.

RAVENSCAR to HAYBURN WYKE

The Route

On leaving the cliffs the path rises up to a cart-track. Go left, and just beyond a lone dwelling we take a right fork to climb steeply through woods. On emerging, a gentler pull leads up to meet a road at Ravenscar. From the crossroads head straight along Station Road, soon taking a track left which ends alarmingly abruptly at the very cliff-top.

From here the Way clings to the top of the steep drop for 3 good miles, much of which is atop the steep and wooded Beast Cliff.

Blea Wyke Point

Common Cliff

74

Coastguard lookout and emergency telephone now vandalised.

path to road railway path

Rocky Point

(92)

Beast Cliff Wood

The walk above Beast Cliff adds a whole new dimension to the Coast Path. Splendid colours are provided by the trees and bracken which rise from far below, right up to the side of the path.

Prospect House Farm

(93)

As height is lost after passing near Prospect House, the view ahead opens up to reveal a distant Scarborough (castle visible though not on skyline), and if clear enough, nothing less than an even more distant Filey Brigg.

Approaching Hayburn Wyke, looking to Tindall Point and Hundale Point

path to 'Stainton-dale Shire Horses'

A beautiful, lonely walk

The Route

As Beast Cliff is tamed we make our first descent to beach-level for over six miles: this is the unmistakeable Hayburn Wyke. A steep drop through trees brings us to the crossing of Hayburn Beck (the second footbridge encountered). From here the tiny detour to the beach waterfall can be made by means of a path after the bridge, with a little scramble down some rocks.

Back on the main path, a climb through more trees follows: keep left at 2 junctions to head back off along the cliff. Two modest indentations occur at Cloughton Wyke and Crook Ness, but the drops are negligible and the way is obvious.

Inland can be seen something of the vast forests which spoil much of the south-east of the National Park.

75

94

Red House Farm

Hayburn Beck

Falls

Hayburn Wyke

Tindall Point

Little Cliff

95

367

96

road -end

to Cloughton

Cloughton Wyke

77

Hayburn Wyke is one of the natural highlights of the Yorkshire coast. Here a delightful wooded valley brings its greenery to the very shore. Added to this are the 'standard' features of rugged cliffs on either side, and the near-unique sight of a waterfall spilling forth onto the rocky beach itself. The area is a nature reserve of the Yorkshire Wildlife Trust.

The waterfall, Hayburn Wyke

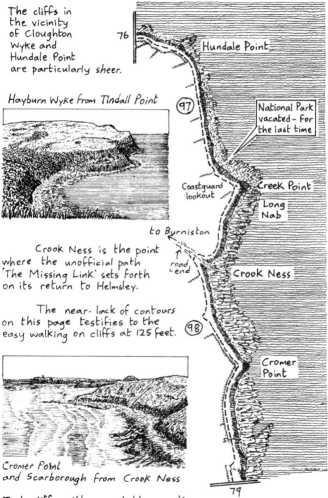

The cliffs in
the vicinity
of Cloughton
Wyke and
Hundale Point
are particularly sheer.

76

Hundale Point

97

National Park
vacated - for
the last time

Coastguard
lookout

Creek Point

Long
Nab

to Burniston

road
end

Crook Ness is the point
where the unofficial path
'The Missing Link' sets forth
on its return to Helmsley.

Crook Ness

The near-lack of contours
on this page testifies to the
easy walking on cliffs at 125 feet.

98

Cromer
Point

Hayburn Wyke from Tindall Point

79

*Cromer Point
and Scarborough from Crook Ness*

Just cliffs - with one notable exception

Scarborough is Yorkshire's major holiday resort and as such boasts a fine assortment of features, of which the standard seaside attractions are only a part. Aside from the slot-machines and candy floss there is much of interest, both historical and modern.

The centrepiece is undoubtedly the castle. Dating from the 12th century it featured prominently during the Civil War, when it was under a long siege. It is also the site of a Roman signal station, and the ruins look down on the town from the mighty headland which divides the two vastly-differing bays. The North Bay is largely free of development: rows of guest-houses stand back from the cliff-top. By contrast the south has much to offer. Here is a colourful harbour with a lighthouse rebuilt after second world war damage. In close proximity sandwiched incongruously between newer buildings is a house where Richard III is reputed to have stayed, and also nearby is a strange former toll-house of 1906. It stands at one end of the Marine Drive, which was completed two years later to link the two bays via the headland. The Drive became free from tolls in 1950.

Climbing the hill behind the south sands is the busy town-centre, and further still there spreads an extensive suburban hinterland, a maze of which we can remain blissfully unaware. Scarborough is in fact a good third in size behind York and Harrogate in the predominantly rural county of North Yorkshire. Between the town centre and the castle is the parish church of St. Mary, dating in part from the 13th century. Here Ann Brontë was buried in 1849.

While still only a fishing port, a spa was established in the 17th century, and this set the town on an up-market course which has never faded. Today Scarborough is a popular conference centre and an even more popular cricketing venue. Its county ground plays host to a famous annual festival of the game.

South Toll House

CROMER POINT to SCARBOROUGH

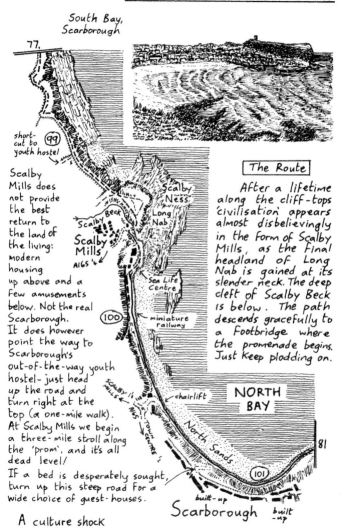

South Bay,
Scarborough

77.

short-cut to
youth hostel

99

Scalby Mills does not provide the best return to the land of the living: modern housing up above and a few amusements below. Not the real Scarborough.
It does however point the way to Scarborough's out-of-the-way youth hostel - just head up the road and turn right at the top (a one-mile walk).
At Scalby Mills we begin a three-mile stroll along the 'prom', and it's all dead level!
If a bed is desperately sought, turn up this steep road for a wide choice of guest-houses.

A culture shock

Scalby
Ness

Long
Nab

Scalby
Beck

Scalby
Mills

A165

Sea Life
Centre

100

miniature
railway

SCALBY MILLS is

chairlift

A165   TOWN CENTRE

NORTH
BAY

North Sands

81

101

built-up

Scarborough   built-up

The Route

After a lifetime along the cliff-tops 'civilisation' appears almost disbelievingly in the form of Scalby Mills, as the final headland of Long Nab is gained at its slender neck. The deep cleft of Scalby Beck is below. The path descends gracefully to a footbridge where the promenade begins. Just keep plodding on.

SECTION 9

———— SCARBOROUGH TO FILEY ————

10 miles   525 feet of ascent

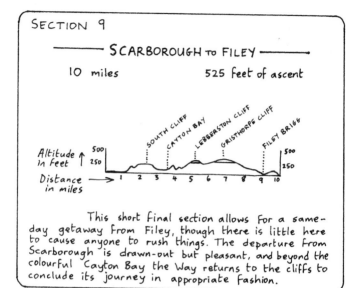

Altitude in feet / Distance in miles — profile showing SOUTH CLIFF, CAYTON BAY, LEBBERSTON CLIFF, GRISTHORPE CLIFF, FILEY BRIGG

This short final section allows for a same-day getaway from Filey, though there is little here to cause anyone to rush things. The departure from Scarborough is drawn-out but pleasant, and beyond the colourful Cayton Bay the Way returns to the cliffs to conclude its journey in appropriate fashion.

Scarborough Castle

SCARBOROUGH to SOUTH CLIFF

The Route

The wide promenade is followed all the way round the North Bay and the headland (always a popular walk) to arrive at the harbour. Keep on around the South Bay past all the amusements until the accompanying road ends at the Spa, just past a roundabout below the imposing Spa Bridge.

Take the path up to the right immediately before the Spa Complex it doubles back through gardens at a steady gradient, sprouting various lesser paths.

On reaching the end of pedestrian-only Spa Bridge, double back up left to gain the Esplanade almost at once. Turn left and head along it, with wooded cliff-gardens on one side and rows of hotels on the other.

Traditional seaside pleasures

The Spa Complex consists of theatre, ballroom and bandstand, and are indelibly linked with the Max Jaffa sound. His orchestra's performances had been the highlight of many 'elder' visitor's holidays almost from time immemorial, but his final summer season ended as the author was passing by to conclude his Cleveland Way journey. Mere coincidence, honest.

Beyond the Spa the promenade extends further still, and a maze of pathways zig-zag up the steep, grassy cliffs. Not all are in good shape however, though that by the lift is fine.

As illustrated opposite, the view from White Nab takes in the remainder of the walk, which isn't really as far as it looks. Don't believe it?

Knipe Point is also known as Osgodby Point after a village inland.

81

Clock Tower

The Esplanade

Scarborough 'cw' sign

SOUTH BAY

Black Rocks

A165

golf course

104

White Nab

Cornelian Bay

Knipe Point

Cayton Sands

CAYTON BAY

SCARBOROUGH A165 22 FILEY 4½

105

83

Beyond Cornelian Bay (named after a type of stone found locally) we encounter one of the few changes in the route of the Way. Originally it had to resort to climbing up to the main road for a stretch, missing the rampant greenery above Cayton Bay.

The memorial clock tower on the Esplanade

Cayton Bay is the last major inlet before Filey Brigg, and its sands, complete with forlorn wartime pillboxes, are a favourite haunt of the crowds from the holiday camp. From here on, uninterrupted chalk cliffs lead to the rocks of the Brigg.

SOUTH CLIFF to CAYTON BAY

The Route

Keep on the Esplanade as far as a clock tower, and here take a pathway through the gardens, at first running parallel with the Esplanade. It then drops down to a path junction by a memorial water-tap: go straight across and up the path climbing left behind it. It soon levels to pass a standard Scarborough authority 'Cleveland Way' sign before resuming as a normal path, joining the cliff-top proper alongside a golf-course.

On entering trees the Way continues in the same direction to reach a junction by modern housing. Go left into the wood and after a right fork a splendid path winds through the trees, emerging into colourful undergrowth above Cayton Bay. Eventually a fence forces the path to climb to a stile near the main road.

[map: CAYTON BAY — Cayton Sands, Cayton Bay, SCARBOROUGH A165 3, FILEY A165, holiday village, 106, Killerby cliff, bunker, 82, 84]

Stay parallel with the road to descend to an access-road and then rise to a cottage by caravans. A short cliff-top section leads to a drive which ends at the last of several dwellings. Now a traditional cliff-top path sends us on our way again.

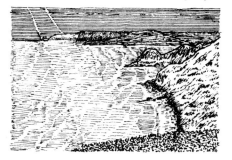

The last lap:
Looking ahead
from White Nab -
Knipe Point,
Red Cliff Point,
Gristhorpe Cliff
and Filey Brigg

A colourful
departure from
the fun

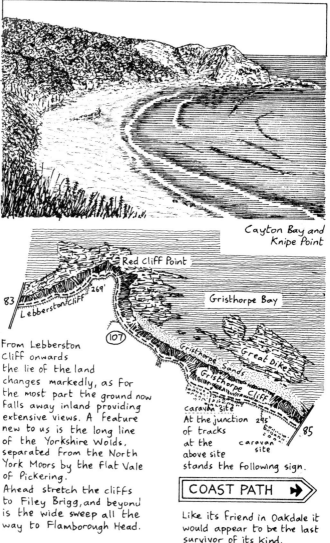

Cayton Bay and Knipe Point

Red Cliff Point

83

Lebberston Cliff 269'

107

Gristhorpe Bay

Gristhorpe Sands

Great Dike

Gristhorpe Cliff

caravan site

At the junction of tracks at the above site stands the following sign.

295'

caravan site

85

From Lebberston Cliff onwards the lie of the land changes markedly, as for the most part the ground now falls away inland providing extensive views. A feature new to us is the long line of the Yorkshire Wolds, separated from the North York Moors by the flat Vale of Pickering.

Ahead stretch the cliffs to Filey Brigg, and beyond is the wide sweep all the way to Flamborough Head.

COAST PATH ➔

Like its friend in Oakdale it would appear to be the last survivor of its kind.

CAYTON BAY to NORTH CLIFF

The Route

The Way now faithfully grips the very cliff-top, rounding Red Cliff Point and soon encountering two caravan-sites. The first encroaches to the cliff-edge, and we make use of its track there-on until it heads inland: the second permits more breathing space. A mile later, the Cleveland Way breathes its last..... but don't stop yet!

84

caravan site · 108

Cunstone Nab

The Wyke

THE OFFICIAL FINISH

Club Point

Yes that's right, the end of the Cleveland Way is marked by nothing more than a stile and a sign warning about the dangerous cliffs (a little late for that). If therefore your life's ambition was to complete the Cleveland Way, you can now fling yourself off the cliff, happy in the knowledge that said ambition has been accomplished. If however, there be more similar ambitions in you, then shelve the celebrations until Filey Brigg is gained. From Newbiggin Cliff to Filey, you are now following the Wolds Way – see overleaf.

Newbiggin's Cliff · 109

North Cliff

87

Gristhorpe Bay, looking to Filey Brigg from Red Cliff Point

Uninterrupted cliff-tops — far from an anti-climax

Filey is a pleasant seaside town with an unruffled air about it, a composed resort - once a spa - sandwiched between the more outgoing Scarborough and Bridlington. The first notable difference is the lack of a harbour: here the fishing cobles are towed to and from their modest landing. The sandy beach is an excellent playground for the bucket-and-spade crew.

The Brigg cuts off the Bay abruptly to the north, while to the south the cliffs regroup and form a wide sweep around to Flamborough Head. After almost the entire way being on the North York Moors, we now find ourselves on the edge of another well-defined area. The Yorkshire Wolds (usually known simply as the Wolds in ignorance of Lincolnshire's equivalent) spread inland from here, and the Wolds Way path crosses their chalk slopes from the Humber to Filey Brigg.

The town itself stands high above the seafront, and incorporates an attractive old fishing quarter. At the top of the Church Ravine stands the parish church of St. Oswald, dating from the 13th century.

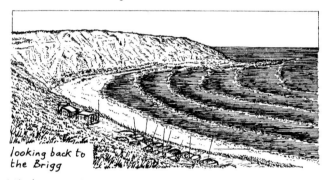

looking back to the Brigg

What a Way to go......

The Cleveland Way's premature demise at a seemingly insignificant location on Newbiggin Cliff is due to a very simple reason. This, you see, is where the old North and East Ridings meet, and the Way was the sole preserve of the former of the two. As North Yorkshire now extends beyond Filey, it would seem sensible to stretch the Way as far as the Brigg. This would appeal even more to Wolds Wayfarers, who at the moment pass through the town to the Brigg, then must (if doing it by the book) go a further mile up the coast before retracing steps back to Filey. At least we're going that way anyway!

NORTH CLIFF to FILEY

The Route

The cliff-path marches on to the neck of land from which Filey Brigg protrudes, and here the well-trodden path from Filey meets us: together we head out to sea. Height is maintained almost to the end of solid land. Now find a suitable grassy couch to relax. For the true enthusiast a path descends to the water-washed reef which can be traced as far out as the North Sea permits.

The way to Filey itself is fairly obvious. Conditions permitting, the rocks at the foot of the Brigg can be used to gain Filey Sands, or alternatively return to the neck of land and follow the tamed cliff-top. A brief descent to a beach-access road precedes a final descent to Church Ravine, and the Coble Landing on the very front.

Note that Filey town appears long before the Brigg is gained

THE LOGICAL FINISH

If you're fortunate enough to have someone waiting to pick you up, this is as good a place as any.

85

North Cliff

110

large car-park in field

Carr Naze

ROAD

miniature golf

111

Filey Sands

Filey Brigg

Church Ravine

THE PRACTICAL FINISH

town centre

112

Coble Landing

FILEY BAY

Filey

A fitting finale- then its off to join the holiday crowds

As the map clearly depicts, Filey Brigg is a thin finger of gritstone protruding into the sea. The Brigg proper is only the outer reef but the term is loosely applied throughout. The upper part, Carr Naze, was the site of a Roman signal station and is a magnificent viewpoint: the coast stretches south to Flamborough Head and north beyond Scarborough.

RECORD OF INNS VISITED

Inn	Location	Comments

....

THE COUNTRY CODE

Respect the life and work of the countryside
Protect wildlife, plants and trees
Keep to public paths across farmland
Safeguard water supplies
Go carefully on country roads
Keep dogs under control
Guard against all risks of fire
Fasten all gates
Leave no litter— take it with you
Make no unnecessary noise
Leave livestock, crops and machinery alone
Use gates and stiles to cross fences, hedges and walls

RECORD OF ACCOMMODATION

Date	Address	Comments

RECORD OF THE JOURNEY

Date	Place	Miles daily	Miles total	Times arrive	Times depart	Comments
	Helmsley	—	1			
	Rievaulx Bridge	3	3			
	Cold Kirby	5½	5½			
	Hambleton	7¼	7¼			
	White Horse	9	9			
	Sutton Bank	1½	10½			
	Sneck Yate	5¼	14¼			
	High Paradise	6¼	15¼			
	Oakdale Head	11¾	20¾			
	Osmotherley	14	23			
	Beacon Hill	2	25			
	Scarth Nick	3	26			
	Huthwaite Green	4¾	27¾			
	Carlton Bank	7¾	30¾			
	The Wainstones	10½	33½			
	Clay Bank Top	11½	34½			
	Round Hill, Urra Moor	1¾	36¼			
	Bloworth Crossing	3	37½			
	Juniper Gate	7½	42			
	Kildale	9½	44			
	Easby Moor	11½	46			
	Gribdale Gate	12¼	46¾			
	Roseberry Topping	14½	49			
	Highcliff Nab	2¼	51¼			

Date	Place	Miles daily	Miles total	Times arrive	Times depart	Comments
	Slapewath	5¼	54¼			
	Skelton Green	7½	56½			
	Skelton	8	57			
	Saltburn YHA	9¼	58¼			
	Saltburn-by-the-Sea	10	59			
	Skinningrove	4	63			
	Boulby Cliff	6¾	65¾			
	Boulby	7¾	66¾			
	Staithes	9¼	68¼			
	Port Mulgrave	10¾	69¾			
	Runswick	12½	71½			
	Kettleness	1¾	73¼			
	Sandsend	5¼	76¾			
	Whitby	8½	80			
	Whitby Lighthouse	10¾	82¼			
	Robin Hood's Bay	15½	87			
	Boggle Hole	½	87½			
	Ravenscar	3½	90½			
	Hayburn Wyke	7½	94½			
	Scalby Mills	12¾	99¾			
	Scarborough Harbour	15	102			
	Scarborough - The Spa	¾	102¾			
	Cayton Bay access road	3¾	105¾			
	Newbiggin Cliff	7	109			
	Filey Brigg	8½	110½			
	Filey	10	112			

INDEX OF PLACE-NAMES ON THE ROUTE-MAPS

INDEX continued

INDEX continued

INDEX continued

Captain Cook's Monument on Easby Moor
looking to Roseberry Topping